S0-BEF-671

Natural Home Gardening

A Practical Guide to Growing
Vegetables for Macrobiotic and
Natural Foods Cooking

By Masato Mimura
With Guidelines by Michio Kushi

One Peaceful World Press
Becket, Massachusetts

Natural Home Gardening
© 1995 by Masato Mimura

All rights reserved. Printed in the United States of America. No part of this book may be used or reproduced in any manner whatsoever without written permission except in the case of brief quotations embodied in critical articles or reviews. For information, contact the publisher.

For further information on mail-order sales, wholesale or retail discounts, distribution, translations, and foreign rights, please contact the publisher:

One Peaceful World Press
P.O. Box 10
Leland Road
Becket, MA 01223
U.S.A.

Telephone (413) 623-2322
Fax (413) 623-8827

First Edition: September 1995
10 9 8 7 6 5 4 3 2 1

ISBN 1–882984–15-3
Printed in U.S.A.

Contents

Foreword

Since early childhood I played in the fields and forests, rivers and oceans, of my native land, Rhode Island. This attraction to nature directed me towards natural foods, macrobiotic diet, and agricultural work. When I started macrobiotic and agricultural pursuits at the age of twenty-one, over twelve years ago, I knew nothing about either. Michio and Aveline Kushi have patiently taught me macrobiotics and given me the opportunity to develop agriculture on their—then recently purchased—558-acre land land in the Berkshire mountains of western Massachusetts.

I began with enthusiasm and no experience, learning many thing the hard way. There were—and still are—rocks, strong weeds, wild animals, biting insects, long cold winters, and droughts. I made many mistakes and the vegetable harvest was small in some years.

For the first five years, I diligently followed Masanobu Fukuoka's natural way of farming. Yet I was unable to produce enough vegetables to feed the rapidly expanding Kushi Institute. Eventually, I realized that natural agriculture, although ultimately very wonderful, was not appropriate because of low yields and difficulty in managing.

Over the years, I have developed methods of cultivating the soil and growing plants based upon ancient traditional methods and the principles of yin and yang. I feel confident enough to present these methods of agriculture to you, so that you can begin to make a garden or improve an old garden and quickly get goodyields of fresh, delicious vegetables without years of trial-and-error.

I am thanful to some of the recent gardeners, farmers, and

authors from whom I have learned such as John Jeavons, Elliot Coleman, Robert Rodale, and Nancy Bubel, and I am in reverence of the countless millions of gardeners and farmers who feed and who have fed the world's population since humanity began.

Let us continue this great and important art as it is inseparable from human life.

Masato Mimura
Brookline, Massachusetts
January 27, 1995

1.
Diet and Agriculture

Diet determines human health. Diet also determines agriculture, including the quantity and quality of food and other agricultural products grown and consumed. The natural environment also helps determine what plants will grow or not grow.

The modern diet consists of large quantities of meat, dairy, eggs, sugar, wheat flour, potatos, and fruit. American agriculture, therefore, consists largely of corn, soybeans, and hay for livestock and wheat, potatoes, sugarcane, and fruit for direct human consumption.

A traditional diet in many parts of Asia, Europe, and Africa consisted of grain, beans, land and sea vegetables, fruit, and fish. Therefore, the agricultural grops were rice, wheat, and other grains, many kinds of beans, many kinds of vegetables, some important fruits, and fish and sea vegetables harvested from the ocean. From an environmental view, raising grain, bean, and hay for animal consumption is inefficient and transporting and importing tropical foods such as sugar, citrus, bananas, and coffee long distances to the north is also counterproductive. To raise 1 pound of beef, a cow must consume about 12 pounds of grain and beans. Therefore, a person who eats 1 pound of beef a day is consuming the equivalent of enough grains and beans that will feed twelve people eating a grain-based diet.

From a dietary and health view, eating meat and eggs daily has been found to be detrimental due to excessive protein,

7

fat, and cholesterol content. Large quantities of refined sugar and chemically preserved and processed foods have also been found harmful. There are numerous other problems created by the modern diet and agricultural system:

1. Soil erosion and depletion from overgrazing and excess plowing to produce high yields to feed animals.
2. Contamination of soil and ground water by agricultural chemicals and manure run off.
3. Deforestation of tropical rain forests to make pastures to raise inexpensive beef.
4. Chemical residues in food.
5. Depletion of deep underwater reserves largely due to the production of livestock food.
6. Farmers in Third World countries are exploited to grow inexpensive cash crops for export such as sugar, tropical fruits, coffee, and drugs.
7. Inhumane treatment of animals, especially beef and dairy cows, chickens, and pigs.
8. Large agribusiness replacing small farmers. (In the U.S. the farm population has dropped to less than 2 percent of the total as a result of this displacement.)
9. Dependency on imported food as a result of agribusiness and lack of local farms and gardens.
10. The art and spirit of farming and gardening are being forgotten and young people do not know the origin of their daily food or how to grow, harvest, process, store, or cook and prepare healthful meals.

In order to change these agricultural problems, the first step is to change our daily diet to one based on whole grains, beans, and vegetables from land and sea. This change will benefit not only our personal health but also the environment.

The macrobiotic dietary approach is a way of eating based on living in harmony with nature. The standard macrobiotic diet created by Michio Kushi and his associates for people living in the temperate climates of the world can easily be modified according to climate, season, weather, age, gender, occupation, condition, and personal needs.

The macrobiotic diet is in harmony with the environment

and human biological evolution. It was practiced in many parts of the world in ancient times and is appropriate for modern humanity. The macrobiotic diet is the foundation for a new agricultural system based on respect for the earth and natural order. Please see the Appendix for a description of the standard macrobiotic diet.

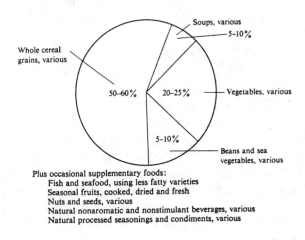

Whole cereal grains, various

Soups, various — 5-10%

50-60%   20-25% — Vegetables, various

5-10%

Beans and sea vegetables, various

Plus occasional supplementary foods:
Fish and seafood, using less fatty varieties
Seasonal fruits, cooked, dried and fresh
Nuts and seeds, various
Natural nonaromatic and nonstimulant beverages, various
Natural processed seasonings and condiments, various

The standard macrobiotic diet is very flexible. An almost infinite variety of meals can be created from the standard suggestions. The amount, volume, and proportion of food in each category may also be adjusted slightly for each person or family member depending upon changing environmental and social conditions. The macrobiotic way of eating allows each person to develop his or her intuition, which is essential to balanced cooking and food preparation, as well as all other aspects of daily life.

The first step in creating a new agricultural system is to change our diet from an animal-based way of eating to one based on grains and vegetables. The second step is for farmers and gardeners to change the crops they grow to ones that support a grain-based diet. For example, corn and soybeans grown for cattle feed can be changed to raising wheat and soybeans for direct human consumption. In the home garden, crops such as potatoes, tomatoes, and eggplant—vegetables of tropical origin usually not eating in temperate latitude macrobiotic homes—can be replaced with more environmentally appropriate crops such as carrots, napa cabbage, and squash. There are many ways in which farmers and gardeners can convert their present crops to crops more fitting to a grain-based and macrobiotic diet. A change in diet and agricultural crops will cause a tremendeous improvement in human health, in agriculture and the economy, and in the environment and planetary health.

After a change of diet and agriculture, the next step is to develop regional agriculture by creating many small, medium, and large farms and gardens. All open areas not designated as natural preserves, roadways, or other work areas can be developed to grow food, fiber, fuel, lumber, and other useful products, thereby reducing the necessity to import large quantities of agricultural products to support the region's population. Each region's farms and gardens would strive for self-sufficiency in producing its own food and other resources, trading its surplus for shortages. For example, coastal regions may produce a surplus of fish, sea vegetables, and sea salt, yet may not be able to produce enough grain and vegetables and therefore would trade with an interior region which has a surplus of these goods and a shortage of sea products. Home gardens are an important part of developing a strong regional agricultural system because each garden can supply a family with about 25 percent of its total food consumption. In addition, gardeners typically share excess vegetables with neighbors, friends, and distant family members.

The fourth major step in creating new agriculture is to grow crops according to organic, sustainable, and more natural type methods. For many thousands of years' people grew crops by organic methods. Chemicals in agriculture are a recent phenomenon, since about the 1940's in America. Although agricultural chemicals appear to grow large yields quickly, they deplete and contaminate the soil which results in lower yields. Organic methods are simple and practical for use on large and small farms and gardens and it is not difficult to convert from chemical farming and gardening to organic methods. The time needed to change most of the world's diet and agriculture may take many years yet there is already a strong movement toward natural foods and organic agriculture in many parts of modern society. The diet may be changed, crops selected and an organic garden set up in one household in a couple of months.

Food connects us with the earth and through food we "eat" the earth and become connected to it. A home garden makes a house a home and makes us more settled in one place. It is a joy to see the garden and vegetables through the seasons. In spring, the soil thaws and is rich and black; scallions, burdock and parsnip leaves emerge from the soil after their long winter dormancy. In summer, many vegetables grow with different colors, shapes and sizes; they grow rapidly with the heat and summer rains. Autumn brings harvests of squash, carrots and onions and other sweet vegetables for winter storage. The soil becomes wet and rich from autumn rains and new compost. The winter garden soil and vegetables rest beneath the snow while pots of rich vegetables cook on the wood stove.

It is not difficult to make a home garden or improve an old garden. Two people working on weekends can set up a fine garden in a couple of months or, working intensively for two weeks, can create an average size garden from even the poorest soil. After the initial construction, maintaining the garden, i.e., harvesting, weeding, watering, etc., require about four hours per week. A home garden creates human health in several ways: first, by the physical activity outdoors in fresh air and sunshine, second, by the fresh organic vegetables harvested and eaten, and, third, by the peace and inspiration created by working and harmonizing with nature.

The vegetables produced will save money and be fresher and more flavorful than store-bought vegetables. Delicious vegetables will enhance meals. Extra ones may be given to neighbors, friends and family.

A well-managed garden is a pleasant place to visit. People of all ages will enjoy it as will various wild animals, birds and insects, and it may increase property value.

Three Types of Agriculture

There are three general types of agriculture currently in practice today; two are widespread and common, one is less known. These three types of agriculture are natural agriculture, organic agriculture and chemical agriculture.

Agriculture is created by heavenly energies such as the sun and the spinning of the earth, by earthly energies such as soil and water, and by human energies such as cultivation and planting. The difference among the three types of agriculture is the degree of human energy involved. Heaven and earth's force (energies) create natural agriculture; human intention and effort are minimal. This type of "agriculture" created the great wild forests and prairies of the world. Masanobu Fukuoka rediscovered natural agriculture methods and wrote several books on the subject. (Reference.) Strict adherence to natural agriculture methods of growing vegetables may not yield enough quantity or variety needed to support a family on a small piece of land. Natural agriculture is not as practical as organic agriculture. In organic agriculture, the farmer and gardener cultivates the land to produce crops yet works closely with heavenly and earthly forces such as the seasons, weather, soil, plants, earthworms, and improves soil using natural or organic materials, hence the name "organic" agriculture.

In chemical agriculture, human intervention is greatest, using new chemicals, machines and techniques to produce the highest yields and highest profits. The intention is usually profit oriented and while the farmer or merchant may become rich, the earth becomes poor. One can convert from chemical agriculture to organic agriculture in about three years. Of the three methods, organic agriculture's farming and gardening is the most practical and balanced for modern society.

2.

Planning a Home Garden

Consider various factors when planning a home garden. Natural and social factors determine the place and size of a garden.

Natural Factors:

1. Movement of the Sun
2. Position of trees
3. Slope of land
4. Position of bodies of water
5. Position of large rocks

Social Factors:

1. Position and size of buildings
2. Position of roads and driveways
3. Boundary lines
4. Position of septic systems
5. Position of electric and telephone poles
6. Position of underground pipes and cables
7. Zoning laws
8. Property ownership
9. Fences

Consider all of these factors when planning a home garden. Most suburban and rural properties have one good place to make a garden.

Natural Factors

Sun

The garden should receive full sun or nearly full sun in the north. In the south, some partial shade may be beneficial. Observe the sun in spring, summer and autumn to determine sunny and shady areas.

Trees

Gardens should be at least 10 feet from trees, the larger the tree the greater the distance should be. Both a tree's branches and roots interfere with a vegetable garden. Tree branches cause shade and roots draw water and nutrients from the soil and make cultivation difficult. Ordinarily we avoid cutting trees, but there are times when cutting some trees and branches will greatly improve a garden area and the health of the remaining trees. (See Forestry for the Home Garden: Chapter Eleven.)

Slope of the Land

Gardens can be made on flat or sloped land. On sloped land, make the garden beds and pathways across the slope of the land (perpendicular to the downhill slope). The North and Northeast sides of hills are least favorable sites for gardens in cold areas because the sun is weakest there, however North and Northeast slopes may be beneficial in hot areas.

Bodies of Water

Bodies of water include rivers, ponds, lakes, swamps, springs and oceans. It is beneficial to have a garden near clean, sweet water. The garden should be beyond normal flooding range should the water rise. Strong wind may blow across a lake and damage vegetables; plants, a fence or row of trees or bushes will correct this problem. Salt water and wind can also damage plants but a double row of evergreen trees and bushes will protect them.

Rock Outcropping

Some areas of the world have large, unmovable rock outcroppings. A successful garden can be made around these if it is the only place available. Plan the garden beds according to the rocks; the beds may be different widths, lengths and shapes. Plan gardens so they will receive full sunlight and make the soil very rich to offset the restrictions created by the rocks.

Social Factors

Buildings

Buildings will block the sun to the garden unless the garden is on the south side or far enough away to be beyond the shadow. Allow 3 feet of space between the garden and building for building maintenance and access to the garden.

Roads and Driveways

Gardens can be made next to small roads and driveways. Set aside a 3-foot space as a pathway in-between the road and the garden bed. A double row of tall bushes or thick trees between gardens and major roads can reduce exhaust and noise from cars.

Boundary Lines

Before making a garden, it is important to know the exact location of all property lines. The garden can be as close as 3 feet to a property line, the 3-foot margin creates a pathway around the garden.

Septic Systems

Most rural and suburban homes will have a septic system consisting of a tank, a leach field and connecting pipes. It is important to know the exact locations of these three parts. A garden should not be made above a tank or pipe or within 12 feet of a leach field. Leave enough room for a septic pump truck to access the tank. Locate the tank by finding the cover; grass grows thick and green over the leach field and the soil may be wet. A 3- or 4-inch diameter connecting pipe will exit a house's basement and go directly to the tank and from the tank directly to the leach field. The septic system is usually downhill and away from the house in an open area.

Electric and telephone poles

Try to avoid making a garden under or around electric and telephone poles and lines, primarily because the utility companies may prohibit this or their trucks may ruin the garden if the electricians need to service the line.

Underground Pipes and Cables

Locate the underground pipes and cables before making a garden. These lines may be water, gas, oil, electric, telephone or sewer; it is best to avoid making a garden over these lines because they may get damaged during cultivation. Also the garden will be ruined if the lines are excavated for servicing.

Zoning Laws

Some areas may prohibit vegetable gardens in front yards and some formal communities may prohibit vegetable gardens altogether. It is helpful to know zoning laws before making a garden.

Property Ownership

Before planning and making a garden, contact the owners of the land and get their permission. A well-tended vegetable garden will add value to a property.

Fence

Around the vegetable garden, in most areas, a fence will be necessary. Make a fence on the boundary line then allow 3 feet for a pathway to the edge of the cultivated soil. Fences can be permanent, semi-permanent or seasonal and can be made of wood, metal or other materials. The following is a sample garden:

The boundary line is in the West, the driveway is in the South and east, and the river and trees in the North determine the size and shape of this garden. The compost site is near the garden and away from the house. The barn, where the tools are stored, is close to the garden.

The home garden is laid out in raised beds (see Chapter 5) 4 feet wide by any length between 8 and 30 feet. Pathways are planned in between the beds (1 to 2 feet wide) and around the periphery, (3 to 6 feet wide). Visualize these beds in the garden area to determine the actual length, direction and quantity of beds and pathways.

A very important part of a home garden is the composting area which should be located in or next to the garden area and some distance away from all houses. It is helpful, but not essential if the compost area is accessible by a road. The compost area can be in an area which is unsuitable for gardening, shade or trees will not greatly affect the compost. To make sufficient quantity of compost for a home garden, an area of at least 10 x 10 feet that is reasonably level is needed. Another area for holding firewood and branches will be needed if tree cutting is to be done.

There are animals in many areas of the world which will eat vegetables from a garden. A fence is the most practical method of keeping them out. When planning the garden, consider a fence set a minimum of 3 feet from the edge of the cultivated soil to allow working space. This wide pathway is in between the periphery of the cultivated soil and the fence.

Gates are placed at convenient locations. A simple and inexpensive fence can be purchased at most farm and hardware stores.

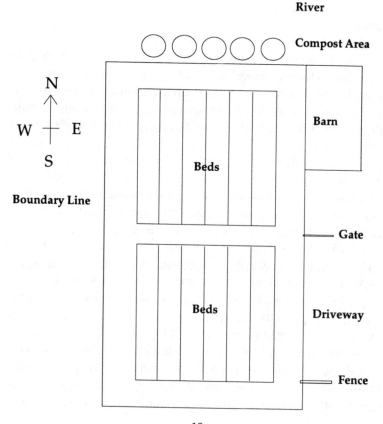

3.
Tools

To make a home garden some tools will be needed; most of the garden work can be accomplished by hand tools. These tools can be purchased at local garden, farm and hardware stores or through mail order companies.

Tools should be kept in good working condition and order and stored in a barn, garage, shed, porch or basement away from weather yet close to the garden area. Wooden tool parts can be sanded and oiled with used cooking oil or linseed oil. Metal parts can be wire-brushed and sharpened with a file. Dull saw blades may be replaced or sharpened. Garden tools, when taken care of, will last many years. All traditional craftsmen and farmers took good care of their tools because it helped them to work efficiently and make high quality products.

There are many types and varieties of tools. For example, among shovels, there are round point, square and broad and these may come in long or short handle varieties. It is important to select the correct tool for the job in order to work efficiently, avoid fatigue and not damage tools, thereby making garden work enjoyable.

The following list of tools are used to make a garden, most homes will already have many of these tools because they are common. Not all of these tools are needed for every garden. For example, soil without large stones will not need a pry bar, soil without roots will not need an ax and most soils will not need a pick ax. Some tools can be made, such as the sifter, wood stakes and stringline.

Spading Fork

A "D" handle tool with four thick tines used for loosening or "forking" soil, one of the most important tools for gardening, imported from England by Smith & Hawken.

Spade

A "D" handle tool with a square flat sharp head used for cutting straight lines in sod and straight lines in trenches.

Shovel

A long handled tool with a rounded and curved head used for digging holes and moving soil.

Wheelbarrow

for transporting soil, compost, manure, stones, limestone, vegetables, leaves, weeds and firewood. An essential tool for a home garden.

Sifter

Made from a 2 'x 3' wood frame covered with wire mesh with 1" holes or larger. Used for sifting topsoil from sod and for sifting course compost.

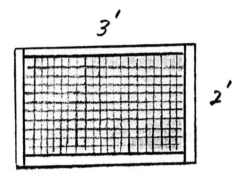

Lawn Mower

This one power tool is very helpful for cutting the grassy area prior to making the garden and for cutting the grass around the garden and in the pathways.

Leaf Rake

A lightweight bamboo or spring steel tool used to remove cut grass from the garden area prior to making the garden and for gathering leaves and other vegetation for use as compost.

Wooden Stakes

About 12 stakes, 18 inches long x 1 inch thick used for planning and marking out garden beds, pathways and fence lines. These can be made from tree branches.

Stringline

50 or 100-foot thin strong nylon string wrapped around a stick, used with the wooden stakes for planning and marking beds, pathways and fence lines.

Tape Measure

A 100-foot ribbon type tape measure is most convenient for setting up a garden. It is used to plan and set up the beds, pathways and fence lines.

Manure Fork

A long handled tool with 5 or 6 long, sharp tines used for turning and moving light, fibrous materials such as manure, compost and grass. This is sometimes called a pitchfork. A hay fork has three long sharp tines and is suitable for hay but not for manure or compost.

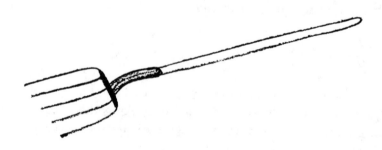

Steel Rake

A long handle tool with a heavy steel head with many short, straight teeth, it is used for leveling garden soil. This is sometimes called a garden rake.

Pry Bar

A long, heavy iron rod used for removing large stones from garden soil.

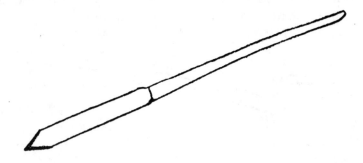

Sledge Hammer

An 8-pound hammer on a long handle is used for breaking large stones in the garden. If the garden soil does not contain large stones, a sledge hammer will not be necessary.

Pickaxe

A long handled tool with a heavy double end sharpened head, used for loosening extremely hard, packed soil such as clay. This tool is not usually needed on sandy or silt soils.

Axe

A tool that is used for cutting tree roots.

Broad Shovel

A long handle tool with a large square head used for moving fine compost, manure, sawdust, limestone or soil.

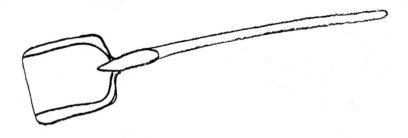

Buckets

Five gallon plastic buckets (which were used to hold food and building materials) are very useful in the garden. Four or more are helpful for holding and transporting soil, limestone, ash, compost, water, weeds, etc.

Cultivator

A long handled tool with four to six long, sharp tines bent perpendicular to the handle, used for mixing compost, manure and limestone into the topsoil.

Collinear Hoe

A long handled tool with a thin, sharp blade used for weeding. This tool is an improvement over the old style hoe; it is lighter and sharper and the angle of the blade makes weeding quick and easy work. Available also in a short-handle, one hand version.

Hori Hori

A knifelike weeding tool (available from Smith and Hawkin).

Tools for Forestry

Bow Saw

A saw with a thin, sharp blade attached to a triangular shaped tube steel frame. Inexpensive, lightweight and sharp, this tool easily cuts trees and branches up to 4 inches wide.

Pruning Saw

A small saw with a narrow blade, used to cut branches off of trees where a bow saw will not fit. It will cut branches that are up to 3 inches in diameter.

Lopping Shears

A long, two handled tool used for cutting small trees, branches and bushes up to 1-inch thick.

Pruning Shears

A small, scissors-like tool used for cutting branches that are up to 1/2-inch thick.

Tools for Planting

Warren Hoe

A hoe with a triangular, steelhead, used for making furrows in the garden soil. Any narrow tool or a strong stick can substitute for a warren hoe.

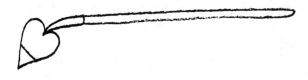

Trowel

A small shovel-like, one hand tool used for making holes in the soil for transplanting vegetables.

Water Can

Used for watering potted plants, transplants and seeds.

4.
Soil, Compost and Fertilizer

To grow vegetables, macrobiotic home gardening uses natural and organic methods rather than artificial and chemical methods. The basis of organic methods of gardening is to make rich, fertile soil by adding organic material in the form of compost.

The way to gain a comprehensive understanding of soil, compost and fertilizer is to use the principles of yin and yang.

The Principles and Laws of the Universe

Traditional cultures have understood the universal principles and laws of change since ancient times and have enshrined them in various ways in their scriptures, myths, systems of agriculture and food production, architecture, and folk arts. In the modern age, various philosophers, scientists, authors and artists have rediscovered and expressed, usually in more fragmented form. In this century, they were comprehensively outlined by George Ohsawa and further simplified by Michio Kushi and his associates through their experiences and observations of nature and society during the past thirty-five years.

We can view the eternal Order of the Universe and understand it in two ways, according to seven universal principles and according to the twelve laws of change. These two perspectives complement each other and we understand them intuitively. We experience them daily wherever we are, always, and under all circumstances.

The seven principles of the infinite universe are:

1. Everything is a differentiation of one Infinity.
2. Everything changes.
3. All antagonisms are complementary.
4. There is nothing identical.
5. What has a front (i.e., a visible side) has a back (i.e., an invisible side).
6. The bigger the front, the bigger the back.
7. What has a beginning has an end.

The twelve laws of change of the infinite universe are:

1. One Infinity manifests itself into complementary and antagonistic tendencies, yin and yang, in its endless change.
2. Yin and yang are manifested continuously from the eternal movement of one infinite universe.
3. Yin represents centrifugality. Yang represents centripetality. Yin and yang together produce energy and all phenomena.
4. Yin attracts yang. Yang attracts yin.
5. Yin repels yin. Yang repels yang.
6. Yin and yang combined in varying proportions produce different phenomena. The attraction and repulsion among phenomena are proportional to the difference of the yin and yang forces.
7. All phenomena are ephemeral, constantly changing their constitution of yin and yang forces; yin changes into yang, yang changes into yin.
8. Nothing is solely yin or solely yang. Everything is composed of both tendencies in varying degrees.
9. There is nothing neutral. Either yin or yang is in excess in every occurrence.
10. Large yin attracts small yin. Large yang attracts small yang.
11. Extreme yin produces yang, and extreme yang pro-

duces yin.

12. All physical manifestations are yang at the center, and yin at the surface.

The terms yin and yang do not represent certain phenomena, nor are they pronouns of certain things. They are showing relative tendencies compared dynamically and therefore are to be understood comprehensively. In daily life on this planet, for example, we experience them in the following ways: in tendency yin is more expansive, while yang is more contracting. In dimension, yin is more spatial, while yang is more temporal. In position, yin is more outward, while yang is more inward. In direction, yin is more ascending, while yang is more descending. In color, yin is more purple, blue and green, while yang is more yellow, brown, orange, and red. In temperature, yin is colder, while yang is hotter. In weight, yin is lighter, while yang is heavier. In natural influence, water results in yin, while fire results in yang.

In atomic structure, electrons and other peripheral particles are more yin, while protons and central particles are more yang. In the world of elements, oxygen, nitrogen, potassium, phosphorous, and others are more yin, while hydrogen, carbon, sodium, arsenic, and others are more yang. In the realm of light, yin is darker, while yang is brighter. In physical construction, yin is more surface and peripheral, while yang is interior and central. In vibration, shorter waves and higher frequency waves are more yin, while longer waves and lower frequency waves are more yang.

In work, yin is more psychological, mental and spiritual in orientation, while yang is more physical, material and social. In attitude yin is more gentle, passive, and receptive, while yang is more aggressive, active, and outgoing. In the biological world, the vegetable kingdom is more yin. In the botanical world, yin manifests as branches, leaves and flowers and plants that are taller, juicier, and more tropical in origin, while yang manifests as roots and stems and plants that are shorter, drier and more northern or colder in origin. In sex, yin is manifests more in female, while yang manifests more in male. In body structures, softer and more expanded organs such as the stomach, intestines and bladder are more yin, while harder and more compacted organs such as the liver, spleen and kidneys are more yang. In the nervous system, peripheral nerves and the orthosympathetic system are more yin, while central nerves and the parasympathetic system are more yang. In taste, spicy, sour and strongly sweet are more yin, while salty, bitter and mildly sweet are more yang. In seasonal influence, hot summer creates a yin expanding influence, while cold winter creates a yang contracting influence.

As we can see, everywhere and in everything, in whole or in part, every manifestation in nature can be observed and experienced, compared and understood, as relatively more yin or more yang, the two antagonistic and complementary forces and tendencies that are constantly harmonizing with each other. The proportion of yin and yang is continually in flux, and yin and yang change constantly into one another. As energy contracts, becomes smaller, and hardens, the pressure of yang increases. Inside motion speeds up, generating heat. When heat is generated, expansion arises. This energy becomes larger, bigger, softer, and slower — more yin. Then as coldness arises, contraction develops and the cycle begins anew. Thus everything eventually turns into its opposite. Hot summer changes into cold winter; youth changes into old age; action changes into rest; the mountain changes into the valley; land changes into ocean; day changes into night; hate changes to love; the rich and powerful decline while the poor and meek prosper; civilizations rise and fall; species come and go; life changes into death and new life is reborn; matter changes into energy; space changes into time; galaxies appear and disappear.

Arising out of Infinity or God, yin and yang are the eternal forces and tendencies governing all phenomena, visible and invisible, individual and group, part and whole, past and future. To know the principles and law of change is to reach the Tree of Life, to drink the water from the River of Life and to live with the justice of the Kingdom of Heaven. When we know these principles and laws, all spiritual and religious concepts, all scientific and philosophical ideas, and all individual and social efforts are unified and understood to be

31

complementary aspects of a larger whole. Across the ages, these principles and laws have been described in various ways and have been known under different names and forms. Understanding them is humanity's greatest achievement. The laws of change and harmony are the natural birthright of us all. Healthy human beings intuitively think and act in terms of yin and yang. These forces and tendencies are a compass enabling us to realize all possible dreams. By knowing them, we can turn sickness into health, war into peace, conflicts into harmony, misery into happiness, chaos into order. They are the invincible, eternal constitution of the infinite universe, as well as of all phenomena within it, including our life and destiny, and all worlds—past, present, and future (see Table I).

	Yin ▽*	Yang △*
Attribute	Centrifugal force	Centripetal force
Tendency	Expansion	Contraction
Function	Diffusion	Fusion
	Dispersion	Assimilation
	Separation	Gathering
	Decomposition	Organization
Movement	More inactive, slower	More active, faster
Vibration	Shorter wave and higher frequency	Longer wave and lower frequency
Direction	Ascent and vertical	Descent and horizontal
Position	More outward and peripheral	More inward and central
Weight	Lighter	Heavier
Temperature	Colder	Hotter
Light	Darker	Brighter
Humidity	Wetter	Drier
Density	Thinner	Thicker
Size	Larger	Smaller
Shape	More expansive and fragile	More contractive and harder
Form	Longer	Shorter
Texture	Softer	Harder
Atomic particle	Electron	Proton
Elements	N, O, P, Ca, etc.	H, C, Na, As, Mg, etc.
Environment	Vibration . . . Air . . . Water . . . Earth	
Climatic effects	Tropical climate	Colder climate
Biological	More vegetable quality	More animal quality
Sex	Female	Male
Organ structure	More hollow and expansive	More compacted and condensed
Nerves	More peripheral, orthosympathetic	More central, parasympathetic
Attitude, emotion	More gentle, negative, defensive	More active, positive, aggressive
Work	More psychological and mental	More physical and social
Consciousness	More universal	More specific
Mental function	Dealing more with the future	Dealing more with the past
Culture	More spiritually oriented	More materially oriented
Dimension	Space	Time

Soil

There are three basic soil types: sand, silt and clay. Soil may be composed of one type only or it may be a mix of two, for example, silty sand or clay silt. These three basic types of soil can be classified by yin and yang;

> Yin: Sand, largest particles, soft and airy
> Silt, medium particles, darker, heavier
> Yang: Clay, smallest particles, heaviest, hardest

Sandy soils tend to be more loose and airy due to the large particle size. Water drains well from sandy soils yet this draining also leaches out some nutrients and causes quick drying out. Sandy soils are frequent in many parts of the world and come in a wide range of colors, particle sizes and mixtures with other soils and stones.

Silt soil particles are smaller than sand particles and usually contain large quantities of organic material which gives it a rich black color and odor when wet. It is usually found in low lying, flat areas near rivers, ponds, lakes or swamps that periodically flood. Silt soils usually do not contain large stones yet often have sand or clay mixed in. It is a highly desirable soil type.

Clay soil particles are the smallest and easily pack together which excludes air. Clay soils become very heavy and sticky when wet and hard when dry. Everyone who has worked with potter's clay will recall these attributes.

Clay soils are common in low lying areas near wide, slow rivers, and can also be found in mountains which were heaved up from low areas. Clay soils are quite fertile yet fertility becomes "locked up" because of the closeness of the soil particles and lack of air. Clay soils come in a wide range of colors and may or may not contain stones.

Good crops can be grown in all three basic soil types and any combination of types. Most soils will improve by adding organic material. Organic material added to sandy soil will fill in the air spaces and make the soil more stable, hold water and hold nutrients. In clay soil, organic material will add air spaces which will help to loosen and drain water when overly wet and loosen and hold water when overly dry. Silt soils will also benefit from organic material because they may be lacking in some major elements due to leaching.

Compost

Compost is composed primarily of yin materials gathered and condensed through heat, time and pressure.

Compost is a very important part of a successful garden and is the basis of organic agriculture. Compost is composed of plant, animal and mineral elements gathered together to ferment and decompose. The digested, broken down material is added to the garden soil for fertilizer for plants. Good compost will contain all the elements vegetable plants need to grow healthy.

There are two basic types of composting material: a yin type and yang type. The following list and descriptions are of the more common and readily available materials:

Yin Compost Elements:

1. Green grass - from mowing the lawn
2. Fresh vegetable waste - from the inedible parts of vegetables
3. Green weeds - all types of weeds with their roots and soil attached
4. Kitchen garbage - any kind of food waste from the kitchen.
5. Manure - from any herbivorous animal such as cow, horse, chicken or rabbit
6. Fresh seaweed - any type, from the sea or freshwater lakes
7. Fish waste - from fish markets or rivers after fish have died from spawning
8. Water - water is an important yin element in the compost pile
9. Air - Air is also an important yin element in the com-

post pile

Yang Compost Elements:

1. Brown grass including hay
2. Straw - straw is the stalk of grain such as rice, wheat or oats
3. Brown leaves from trees in autumn
4. Brown weeds; old, dry, hard weeds
5. Sawdust - from lumber mills
6. Soil - any soil without stones
7. wood ash - from clean wood, i.e., wood that has no paint, nails or glue
8. Dry seaweed - older seaweed which has become hard and dry from the sun
9. Rock powders - from limestone and granite, etc.
10. Grain hulls - from grain milling companies

There are many other types of materials suitable for composting which may be located near the garden site such as old leaf piles, grass piles, vegetable markets, and food processing shops.

Nearly all materials can be classified as more yin type or more yang type materials depending on their water, mineral, protein, carbon and air content. With some experience, gardeners will know intuitively whether a material is of the yin type or yang type. This is important to know when building a compost pile.

There are a few materials which should not be added to a compost pile, for example, wood branches or wood chips in large quantities because both of these materials decompose very slowly. Another material to avoid is the waste from meat eating animals such as cats and dogs; this is very yin material due to its high protein content and odor which attracts parasite animals that are also compatible to the human body.

Periodically, domesticated animals such as cows and horses may be given unnatural foods or medicines. Some of this material may pass through their intestine into the manure; however, any artificial chemicals or elements will fully decompose in the compost pile and further more decompose in the garden soil so that there will be no trace in the vegetables themselves. Fresh manures should not be put near growing vegetables.

Animal manures are not absolutely essential; however, they are usually available in large quantities and free for hauling away. They quickly improve garden soil and make good compost piles.

The animal, plant and element kingdom are inseparable. There are animals of all sizes living in and on the soil leaving manure and their bodies, after they die, to decompose which improves the nutritional quality of the soil, therefore, improves plant growth. Without adding manure from horses, cows or chickens, manure is in the soil naturally.

Compost site and structure: A good place for a compost area is a level area near the garden, away from the house, out of sight, accessible by truck, car or wheelbarrow, partly shady and on firm, dry soil, not soft and wet.

There are many structures and containers for composting. These are two of the simpler, more practical and economical ones:

First is a simple pile of about 6 feet in diameter and 4 to 5 feet high. This method is good except that the outside materials do not compost well and animals may pull the pile apart in search of food. A better method is to make wooden bins from shipping pallets. Three bins is a minimum, 4 or 5 is better and will allow more compost to be produced and allow more time for materials to decompose before being removed:

Four pallets are needed for the first bin and three for each additional bin. Set the pallets vertically and secure with two pipes or stakes per pallet. The pallets may be cut to make them shorter which will make turning and filling easier. The back corners can be tied together to make the bin more sturdy, the front pallet should be able to lift off easy for turning and unloading.

To start a compost pile, add layers of different types of materials in about 3-inch layers (soil and ash and rock powder in 1/2" layers). Alternating yin type and yang type materials will make the best compost; however, it is not absolutely

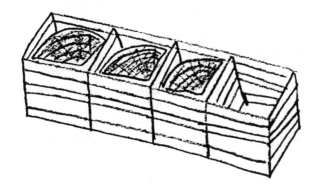

necessary because air and water are throughout the pile. Also, turning the pile later will mix both types together. Using whatever materials are available, build a large pile or fill one bin. If materials are dry, add water; if materials are wet, add something dry like sawdust or leaves.

The pile should heat up to 100 degrees F. to 150 degrees F. With a fork or shovel, check inside the pile in three days to see or feel if it is hot. Most piles will heat up even in cold weather. The pile can be turned in one to two weeks. Using a five-tine manure fork, transfer the compost from one pile to another or from one bin to another, mixing and shredding materials. The top goes to the bottom, outside to the inside, bottom to the top, inside to outside. This insures that all the material spends time in the center of the pile.

Two basic problems can arise from compost that is improperly made. One is a yin condition that is caused by too much water (yin) or wet material (yin). This prevents air getting to the pile and a foul order will arise (yin); the compost will be cold and slimy (yin). For this problem, add something yang to absorb the water and stabilize the pile—brown leaf, sawdust or hay works best. The other problem that may occur in a compost pile is from a yang condition caused by too much hard, dry material and not enough yin material. This type of pile will be cold, dry and odorless. It will decompose naturally yet it will take a long time. To speed up the decomposing in this type of pile, add manure, green grass or weeds and water while turning and mixing.

The pile can be turned a second time after one to two weeks and a third time after another two weeks. Compost will reduce in volume by 65 percent after the third turning and mixing. The speed at which compost breaks down is determined by:

1) Coarseness of the material. (Fine material will break down sooner.)

2) Proper ratio of yin and yang materials, i.e., not too dry and hard and not too wet

3) Frequency of mixing - frequent mixing will speed up decomposing

4) Air temperature - faster decomposing in summer, slower in winter

One to two weeks after the third mixing and turning, the compost can be used in the garden or it can sit and wait. It may still be course yet it will be black and have no strong odor or excess heat.

Fertilizer

Fertilizer is any kind of natural or synthetic material added to soil to increase its fertility or nutrition. Plant nutrition can be compared to human nutrition. The three major elements essential to plant growth, as explained by plant scientists, are nitrogen (N), phosphorus (P) and potassium (K). Organic farmers will also include organic material (Og.), mineral (M) and material which alkalizes soil (pH). Water and air, although not technically fertilizers, are also very important to soil and plant life. Nutritional scientists consider protein, carbohydrates and minerals as essential parts of human nutrition.

This is a comparison of plant and human nutritional elements:

Plant Food	Human Food
Nitrogen (N)	Protein
Phosphorus (P)	Carbohydrates
Potassium (K)	Mineral (Sodium)

Organic material including compost contains all three elements and would be like a balanced meal to humans.

Like human blood, soil also has an acid and alkaline balance. Certain yang type materials will alkalize acidic soil just as salt will alkalize human blood. These materials will alkalize soil:

1. Limestone - ground white stone which contains calcium and magnesium
2. Wood ash - from clean wood
3. Seaweed powder - usually from kelp, dried and crushed.

Limestone and wood ash may be applied directly to the garden at 50 lbs. per 100 sq. ft. And seaweed powder at 25 lbs. per 100 sq. ft plus 25 lbs. limestone or wood ash.

The acid and alkaline scale goes from 0 to 14; O is very acidic and 14 very alkaline. Soil for vegetables should be in the 6 to 7 range or slightly acid. This is called soil pH. pH mans "potential of hydrogen."

A new gardener may wish to have the soil tested in a new garden. Soil test kits can be purchased from agriculture stores, hardware stores, garden sections of department stores or through seed company's mail order or the soil may be tested at the soil test lab at most universities.

The following is a list of common compost materials and the major elements they contain:

og = (organic)
Compost: N-P-K-Og-MIN...
Manure: N-P Og
Brown leaf: Og
Green grass: N Og
Brown grass: Og

Seaweed: K MIN. ALK
Limestone: MIN. ALK
Fish waste N
Sawdust   Og
Wood ash K   ALK
Straw   Og

Compost contains small amounts of all elements and large amounts of organic material which continues to decompose and become phosphorus (P). Organic material in compost also feeds the earthworms which deposit worm castings or manure, i.e., nitrogen (N). Compost and organic materials absorb water and hold it and release it slowly to plants when the weather becomes dry. Compost also holds air in the soil which is essential to plants and soil animals.

5.
Double Digging

Double digging is the basic method of cultivation used in creating a home garden. It is an ancient method used in Europe, Asia and Central America. It is most suitable in areas with poor agricultural quality such as mountainous areas, rocky soils, dry sandy soils, cold areas, and wet areas. Double digging is also suitable on small properties such as the average American home property and in highly populated areas where land is scarce. It is also a good method in countries that are poor, heavily populated and have no money for expensive machinery.

Double digging does not require any machinery except for a vehicle used to haul materials for compost and soil enrichment. Garden beds may be double dug one time only and thereafter maintained by weeding, harvesting the crop and fertilizing with compost or manure. If, however, the beds are walked on and are not weeded and refertilized after the crop is harvested, they may need to be dug again to get maximum results.

The name, double digging, comes from the two-part step of cultivating the topsoil and the subsoil that naturally forms a raised mound or "bed." Double dug beds warm up quickly in the spring and yet also hold moisture inside during the heat of summer. Before starting the process of double digging, determine the position, size and quantity of beds according to a garden plan.

The width of the beds is 4 feet. This width allows a person to reach the center of the bed with their hands without standing on or in the bed. Not walking in the bed allows the soil to stay soft and promotes large, healthy plant roots.

The size of the property determines the length yet about 8 feet is minimum and about 25 feet is maximum. Beds longer than 25 feet are hard to walk around to get to the other side, during garden work.

The width of the pathways between the beds can be about 20-24 inches to accommodate an average lawn mower if grass is growing between the beds. The minimum width between beds is 12 inches or 1 foot. With this spacing, you may remove the grass between the beds, leaving bare soil.

The pathways around the periphery of the beds should be a minimum of 3 feet to accommodate a wheelbarrow for a small garden or 5 to 10 feet to accommodate a vehicle for a large garden.

The type of vegetation covering the soil determines the preparation for double digging. In most places the vegetation is grass or sod, like a typical American yard, or a grass and weed mix as in a place that has not been mowed frequently. Step by step preparation:

1. Cut and rake the whole area clean with a lawnmower and rake. Use the cut material in the compost.

2. Drive wooden stakes into the ground at the corners of the beds, allowing for 2-foot wide pathways and 4-foot wide beds. The length may be between 8 feet and 25 feet average.

3. Attach a string at ground level to one stake and then around the periphery of the bed, thus forming a rectangle.

4. Apply limestone (a white rock powder made from crushed lime, the same material used on baseball fields) along (on top of) the string then remove the string and the stakes. This results in a white rectangle.

5. Cut along the white line using a spade (a narrow, square, flat and sharp shovel-like tool) cutting through the roots of the grass or sod.

6. Cut the sod into pieces small enough to pick up, for example, 1 foot x 2 feet.

7. Pick up the pieces of sod, roots and grass, with a spading fork and sift the soil out of the roots of the sod. Use a

piece of wire mesh or wire fence that has holes at least 1 x1 inch—yet holes that are larger, for example 2 x 2 inches will allow the soil attached to the roots to fall off more quickly thereby making this step go more quickly and easily. The frame for the wire mesh should be about 2 feet x 3 feet and made of wood. Set this upon a wheelbarrow, a cart, or over two sawhorses. Return all this soil to the bed, remove any large stones, such as stones the size of a tennis ball and larger, and put them in the area designated as a stone dump. Take the sod to the compost area; it will be used to make compost.

8. After the sod has been removed, loosen the top 10 inches with a spading fork. This is called "forking." Stand in the bed and work backwards. Remove stones that are larger than tennis balls; after this step, avoid walking on the bed so that the soil does not become compacted.

9. Add compost to the bed. If the soil is naturally rich, 3 inches of compost is sufficient, if the soil is poor then add 4 to 5 inches of compost. This compost should be of a fine texture, especially if vegetables will be planted soon after. Use course compost, fresh manure or fresh organic material, such as leaves if the beds are prepared in the autumn in areas that have winters. The course material will break down sufficiently by spring planting time.

10. Standing in the pathway, remove the topsoil from the first trench about 10-12 inches deep and about 18 inches wide, or two shovels' width. Use a shovel and place this topsoil into a wheel-barrow. The compost that is on this topsoil will become mixed with the soil as it is put into the wheelbarrow.

11. Put the wheelbarrow at the other end of the bed to use in the last trench. Do not take subsoil up into the topsoil; it is better to leave a little top soil on the subsoil. The color of the subsoil will be different from the color of the topsoil.

12. Loosen the soil in the bottom of this first trench with a spading fork to the depth of 10 to 12 inches. This is called "forking the subsoil." Remove any large stones, add 6 inches of course compost, manure, or course organic material and mix this material into the subsoil. Course material is suitable in the subsoil; it will not interfere with seeds or sprouts as it would in the topsoil. However, it's best to allow fresh manure

to decompose about a month before planting.

13. Cover the first trench subsoil with the topsoil from the second trench. The second trench is the same width as the first trench, about 18 inches or two shovel widths.

14. Fork the subsoil in the second trench in the same way as the first trench, remove stones, add 6 inches of organic material and mix.

15. Cover the subsoil in the second trench with the topsoil from the third trench and continue this process to the last trench.

16. Place the topsoil from the wheelbarrow on the subsoil of the last trench.

17. Rake the bed smooth with an iron rake; the bed can be flat topped or rounded. The rounded form creates more growing space than the flat top form. The flat top formed is good on beds that go across steep slopes as they will form small terraces.

18. The bed is now ready to plant seeds or transplants or cover with mulch for winter. Two people can prepare, dig and plant a 4 foot by 20 foot bed in one day if they have the tools and compost materials available at the garden site.

Sometimes there are large stones in the soil; pry them out with a long iron bar called a pry bar. A fork or shovel will break if used to pry out large stones.

When digging and prying out large stones, try not to lose the sequence and order of the trenches, topsoil and subsoil. Form the beds around extremely large, unmovable stones. If a large stone is deep in the subsoil, disregard it and leave it where it is. Some large stones may be broken with a sledge hammer along a weak line on the stone.

The double digging method is also suitable in an established garden, to make double dug beds:

1. Rake the garden clean in the spring or autumn after the last crops are harvested.

2. Plan and mark the beds and pathways

3. Shovel the soil from the narrow interior pathways onto the beds

5. Double dig as usual

The double digging method is also suitable in areas with good soil; the process will go more quickly and easily. A home garden can be as large as a half acre in good fertile soil on flat land; however, this method does not replace large-scale, mechanized farming which is practical on fields of 1 acre and more.

		(Compost	Step #9)		
Remove topsoil	(Step #10)				
Loosen subsoil	(Step #12)				

Sideview

Trench 1st   2nd   3rd   4th   5th

Remove topsoil and compost from 1st trench (Step #10)	After loosening 1st trench subsoil add compost and cover with 2nd trench topsoil	Continue		

1st trench compost and topsoil is put on top of last trench subsoil

Topview

About 18" wide trenches

45

6.
Planting

The most practical crop to grow in a home garden is vegetables. Vegetables comprise 20-30 percent of the macrobiotic diet. Growing grain in a small garden is not as practical as growing vegetables. If a home garden is very large, one can grow dry beans practically as well as some smaller type fruits like strawberries, blueberries and raspberries, however growing a small patch of grain for the purpose of one's education is practical.

The origin of present day vegetables was from wild vegetables. Modern agriculture began about 12,000 years ago with the cultivation of grains, beans, vegetables, seeds and fruits, also the domestication of animals. All of these crops were originally wild and natural. A vegetable plant was harvested from the wild place. As it was harvested more frequently, it became scarcer and people had to travel further from their home to find it. Then people gathered the seeds and roots of the vegetable plant and planted them near their home in an open place with good soil. They removed weeds and watered the plants. Each year they added new types of vegetable plants and saved the seeds of the best plants to replant in the spring. These original gardeners selected plants according to their special qualities for example; radishes that grow large and keep well into winter, squash which has a very sweet flavor or peas that bears many large peas and grows well in cold weather. Natural selection is the method of choosing the best plant's seeds for replanting; this is why wild radish is different from domestic type radishes. This process of natural selection is still practiced today. Seeds from natural selection are also called "open pollinated" or "standard." Open pollinated seeds are the first choice of seeds for the home garden. By choosing open pollinated seed, the gardener has the option of naturally selecting vegetable plants and their seeds to plant the next year. Hybrid is a modern type seed and is indicated by "F-1" on the seed pack or catalog. "F-1" means "first filial" and is the result of crossing two distinctly different varieties of a certain type of vegetable to produce an offspring (first filial) that has superior qualities than its two parents. Although the body or fruits of the first filial vegetable plant may be exceptionally good, its seed, (offspring) will not have the same qualities, and most likely will become a very odd plant. For example, there is an early maturing, cold-resistant, daikon radish, yet it is small and the flavor is not very good, and there is an open pollinated, large, very flavorful daikon radish, yet it is late maturing and not cold hardy. Plant breeders then artificially cross breed the flowers of these two distinctly different varieties of daikon and produce F-1 seed, which is "early maturing, cold-resistant, large and flavorful daikon radish." This is apparently a wonderful daikon; however, the seed can not be saved and replanted. New seed must be bought each year and it is usually more expensive than standard open pollinated seed.

Most vegetables grown by commercial farmers and about half grown by organic farmers are hybrid (F-1) vegetables.

When selecting crops and varieties, it is important to select crops that will grow and mature properly in the area they are planted. For example, no farmer would grow rice in New England because summers are too short and cold, yet wheat or rye is a practical crop.

Variety refers to one variation of a certain crop. For example, there is "nantes" carrots (long and thin) and "danvers" carrots (medium and thick). When reading the seed catalogs, to choose a variety remember that no variety is good or bad or better than another. Each variety has its' certain qualities and no variety is perfect in every way. It is good practice to plant two varieties of each vegetable each year, and replant the variety that is most suitable to the environmental condition and the gardeners need; then compare the chosen variety with a new variety each year. After a few years, most gardeners will find a core of their favorite varieties. Different seed companies offer different (and some of the same) varieties. There are many, many varieties of each kind of vegetable. For example, cucumbers alone may be fifty different varieties offered by seed companies in the US alone. This includes OP and Hybrid.

The following is the crop list of vegetables grown at the Kushi Institute listed in three alphabetized columns based upon order of importance. This crop list has been carefully selected and tested according to:

1. Michio Kushi's dietary recommendations for people living in a four-season climate.
2. The preference of the Kushi Institute's cooks over the last ten years for flavor, color, etc.
3. What will grow successfully in this climate and geographical location.

The home gardener is not limited to these vegetables and may try a wider variety of vegetables including green soybean, Kohlrabi, escarole, chicory, endive, shallots, horse radish, green beans, watercress and others according to climate, geographical location, personal tastes and condition.

Before planting, the gardener must find the dates of some important natural phenomena, using the chart on page 49 for northern latitude and (the high southern latitudes in the Southern hemisphere). Hot climates without snow in winter may have totally different dates.

To determine the dates of each natural phenomenon, ask an older person who has lived in the area for many years or a local farmer. The dates in parentheses represent Becket, MA (42.5 N latitude 73.5 E and elevation 1300 ft.), which is a cold, four-season climate.

Based on these important dates (page 49) the vegetables from the crop list (page 49) are put into the "planting guideline" (page 50). This planting plan is a guideline to help the gardener know when and how to plant.

Crop List for Northern Climates

Primary	Secondary	Tertiarty
Broccoli	Bok choy	Arugula
Broccoli rabe	Brussels sprout	Chive
Burdock	Celery	Dandelion
Cabbage	Cucumber	Shiso
Carrot	Lettuce	Shungiku
Cauliflower	Mizuna	
Collard	Mustard	
Daikon	Parsley	
Kale	Parsnip	
Leek	Pea	
Napa	Radish	
Onion	Rutabaga	
Scallion	Stringbean	
Squash	Summer Squash	
Sweet Corn	Turnip	

Calendar of Important Dates

Summer
Active Harvest

Last Frost
Plant frost
tender crops
(June 1)

Soil Thaws
1st direct plant-
ing (April 15)

1st Flats Planting
6 weeks before
soil thaws
(March 1)

Last Major Planting
8 weeks before
last plant
growth (July 15)

First Frost
(Sept. 1)

Last Plant Growth
(Sept. 15)

July
June   Aug.
May   Sept.
April   Oct.
Mar.   Nov.
Feb.   Dec.
Jan.

Soil Freezes
Last Harvest

Winter
Planning and Rest

Planting Guidelines

Direct = D Flats = F Transplant = T

Crop & Variety	Frost Hardy Frost Tender	March	April	May	June	July
Broccoli	FH	F	F, T	F, T	F, T	F, T
Broc. Raab	FH	—	D	D	D	D
Burdock	FH	—	D	D	—	—
Cabbage	FH	F	F, T	F, T	F, T	T
Carrot	FH	—	D	D	D	D
Cauliflower	FH	F	F, T	F, T	F, T	T
Collard	FH	F	F, T	F, T	F, T	F, T
Daikon	FH	—	D	D	D	D
Kale	FH	F	F, T	F, T	F, T	F
Leek	FH	F	T	—	—	—
Napa	FH	F	F, T	F, T	F, T	F, T
Onion	FH	F	T	—	—	—
Scallion	FH	F	T	D	D	D
Squash	FT	—	—	F	T	—
Sweetcorn	FT	—	—	—	D	—
Bok Choy	FH	F	F, T	F, T	F, T	F, T
Brussel Sp.	FH	F	T	—	—	—
Celery	FH	F	T	—	—	—
Cucumber	FT	—	—	F	F, T	T
Lettuce	FH	F	F, T	F, T	F, T	F, T
Mizuna	FH	F	F, T	F, T	F, T	F, T
Mustard	FH	F	F, T	F, T	F, T	F, T
Parsley	FH	F	T	—	—	—
Parsnip	FH	—	D	—	—	—
Pea	FH	—	D	D	D	—
Radish	FH	—	D	D	D	D
Rutabega	FH	—	D	D	D	—
Stringbean	FT	—	—	—	D	D
Summer Sq.	FT	—	—	F	F, T	T
Arugula	FH	F	F, T	F, T	F, T	F, T
Chive	FH	F	T	—	—	—
Dandelion	FH	F	F, T	F, T	F, T	F, T
Shiso	FT	—	—	F	T	—
Shungiku	FH	—	F	F, T	F, T	F, T

Planting Guidelines

Direct = D Flats = F Transplant = T

Aug.	Rows Per Bed	Plant/Seed Distance	Depth/direct planting	Notes	Crop & Variety
T	3	15"	—		Broccoli
—	4	3"	1/2"	thin to 10"	Broc. Raab
—	3	4"	1/2"	thin to 8"	Burdock
—	3	15"	—		Cabbage
—	4	1"	1/4"	thin to 1-2"	Carrot
—	3	15"	—		Cauliflower
T	3	15"	—		Collard
—	4	3"	1/2"	thin to 8"	Daikon
T	3	15"	—		Kale
—	4	12"	—	3 plants in a	Leek
T	3	15"	—	bunch	Napa
—	4	4"	—		Onion
—	5	1"	1/2"	may use sets	Scallion
—	1	3 ft.	—	perennial	Squash
—	2	15"	1"	variety	Sweetcorn
T	4	12"	—		Bok Choy
—	2	18"	—		Brussel Sp.
—	4	12"	—	slow germi-	Celery
—	2	15"	—	nation	Cucumber
T	4	8-12"	—	iceberg spac-	Lettuce
T	4	10"	—	ing12"	Mizuna
T	4	10"	—		Mustard
—	5	8"	—	slow germina.	Parsley
—	4	2"	1/2"	thin to 2-3"	Parsnip
—	4	3"	1"	no thinning	Pea
D	6	1"	1/2"	no thinning	Radish
—	3	2"	1/2"	thin to 5"	Rutabaga
—	4	4"	1"	no thinning	Stringbean
—	1	3 ft.	—		Summer Sq.
T	5	6"	—		Arugula
—	6	8"	—	perennial, di-	Chive
T	5	8"	—	vide roots	Dandelion
—	4	12"	—	low seed	Shiso
T	4	8"	—	germination	Shungiku

Explanation of Planting Guide

This planting guide is to help the gardener keep track of the important information needed to plant flats, direct plant, and transplant. A gardener can adjust this guide to his particular climate and needs. For example, warmer climates may add the months of February and September to the guide and may delete any easily memorized information such as "frost hardy" and "planting depth" information. This guide is a sample of ways of planting in Becket, Mass., or any four-season climate.

Column 1— Crop and Variety—lists the vegetable crop and the varieties to be planted

Column 2—Frost Hardy (FH) and Frost Tender (FT)— enter FH if plants can tolerate a frost or FT if a plant can not tolerate a frost

Column 3-8—The months from earliest to latest possible planting. Enter "flats" (F) if flats are started in that month; enter "direct" (D) if seeds are direct planted in that month, and enter "transplant" (T) if transplanting is to be done in that month.

Column 9—Rows per Bed—Based upon a 4 foot wide bed, this is the correct number of rows to make down the length of the bed.

Column 10—Plant or Seed Distance—Enter the distance a plant is transplanted on in the row or the distance between seeds when direct planting.

Column 11—Depth of Direct Planting—Enter the depth in which a seed should be covered with soil.

Column 12—Notes—Enter any special information needed for accurate planting; for example thinning of plants.

Direct Planting

After a bed has been double dug and raked smooth, seeds may be planted, according to the correct time, step by step:

1. Decide how many feet of the bed will be planted to a

certain crop, i.e., a 4 foot by 20 foot bed will be 5 feet to carrots, 5 feet to burdock, 5 feet to parsnips and 5 feet to turnips.

2. Decide how many rows are needed for the crop to be planted. Carrots will require four rows so make four straight rows or furrows 5 feet long with a warren hoe or similar narrow hoe (a stick or tool handle will also work). A furrow is a long narrow shallow trench about 1-1/2 inches deep. the four furrows should be about one foot apart and six inches from the edge of the bed.

3. Place one carrot seed per inch in all four furrows along the five foot length. One method of planting small seed is to put the seed in a heavy bowl, take a pinch of seed between thumb and index finger and rub and roll the finger tips allowing seed to slowly fall out while moving the hand horizontally along the furrow. Large seeds, such as daikon and burdock can be picked up from the bowl one to three at a time and dropped in the furrow.

4. Cover the seed with soil according to recommendations, i.e., carrots should be covered by about 1/4". Keep stones and other course material from covering the seed, as this will obstruct the sprout from rising to the surface.

5. Write on a small piece of wood the name of the crop, variety, and date of planting. Set this marker at the beginning of the planted area.

This information will help the gardener learn more about varieties and planting dates.

Flats and Transplanting

Starting seeds in pots with good soil in a warm sunny place, and with water, gets plants off to an early start. Harvest may come up to four to six weeks sooner with transplanting over direct planting the same crop.

Not all crops are suitable for transplanting. Root vegetables are direct planted. Transplanting allows the gardener to manage the three major factors of plant growth; when the plants are young and fragile, those three factors are soil, sun and water. Transplanting also lengthens the growing period for long season crops such as squash.

The first step in the transplant method is to make or buy potting soil. There are many potting soil recipes. A simple recipe that works well is 50 percent compost and 50 percent soil. The compost should be aged at least six months and sifted through a 1/2 inch or 3/8 inch wire mesh sifter to remove large debris. The soil should be good black topsoil also sifted through a 1/2 inch or 3/8 inch wire mesh sifter. If this is not available, a good potting soil from the local hardware, farm or garden store can be used.

There are also many kinds of pots, the most common types are plastic pots. The 2 inch to 3 inch in diameter size is best for vegetables. The pots, round or square, should fit into a tray or box that will hold 10-12 or 20. These trays of pots are called "flats."

Step by Step Flats Transplanting

1. After selecting the flats, fill each pot with moist potting soil, tap the pot to settle the soil, and fill to 1/4" from the top.

2. With a finger, push a hole into the center of each pot about 1/4 inch deep.

3. Place two seeds into each hole, i.e., two seeds per pot (Note: squash seeds are large, therefore require a larger and deeper hole than 1/4 inch.) If the seed has poor germination or if it is old, up to 5 seeds may be put in 1 pot.

4. Cover the seeds lightly with about 1/4 inch of soil (large squash seeds 1/2")

5. Write the name of the crop , variety, and the date on a small piece of wood or cardboard in pencil, and insert it near the pots. One flat may contain several crops and varieties or may be all one crop and variety.

6. Water the flats with a fine sprinkle of warm water. A watering can with small holes works best.

7. For early spring planting of flats, place the flats in a warm sunny place such as a window, a porch, or outside against a south facing wall. A simple "cold frame" can be made from a window set against a wall or upon blocks with

the flats inside protected from the cold wind. Flats can be taken inside at night when the temperatures drop below freezing. For summer and autumn flats, the flats can stay outside, however right after planting, the flats should be put in a cool shady place to germinate because the hot summer sun will soon dry out the soil and young sprouts. After the seeds have all germinated and have leaves, the flats can be put in the sun. Extreme hot, bright sun and strong rains cam damage young plants, therefore some protection is beneficial such as a covered porch or under the eaves of a house during rain storms.

8. Water late spring flats and summer flats generously keep the soil moist, yet not soaking wet. Too much water on early spring flats will cause a fungus that may kill the young plants.

9. Fertilize with a liquid fish-kelp fertilizer once every week or two (see reference Johnny's Seed Co.) This is necessary because the pot is a closed container and the plant roots are without access to the unlimited space and nutrients of the real earth. A "tea" can be made from compost to fertilize flats which will substitute for fish-kelp fertilizer. To make "compost tea," place one shovel full of finished compost in a burlap bag, tie it shut, and soak it in a bucket of water for twenty-four hours. Remove the bag and squeeze out the excess water. Use this dark liquid to water the flats. It can be made once every week or two.

10. Thin the flats to one plant per pot when the plants are about 1 inch high and have two leaves. Select the most healthy plant and pull out or pinch the other plant. If two plants remain, than both plants will be small and weak. The exception to this is multiple-plant pots such as scallion, leek and chive, which can have four plants per pot. (This is indicated on the planting plan).

11. Transplant to the garden raised beds when the plants are about 4 inches tall or four to six weeks old. Spring planted flats will grow more slowly than summer planted flats. Transplant on a still, but cloudy day, when rain looks probable. Wind can damage young plants, as can bright sun. If plants must be planted during sunny weather, late afternoon is best because the cool night and dew will come soon afterwards. In

other words, yin type weather conditions are preferable due to the yang shock of getting transplanted.

Note the number of rows needed for the crop to be transplanted and the distance between the mature plant. For example, broccoli requires three rows and 15 inches between each mature plant. Make a hole with a stick every 15 inches along three rows, with the holes off-set from each other in each row.

Direct Planting and Transplanting

Example of transplanting at 15" spacing

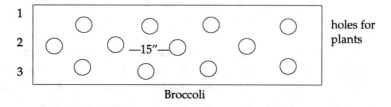

Broccoli

Examples of direct planting 3 rows—1" seed spacing

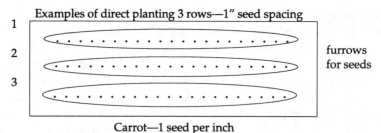

Carrot—1 seed per inch

Making holes can be done while standing and walking along the bed putting holes in the center row and then the row nearest. Then make holes on the other sides of the bed. If the spacing or pattern of the holes does not look right, merely "erase" them and do it again. This hole is only marking the place of the plant. Water the flats well, then set the flats on the bed. Open a hole with a trowel or bare hand to about 3 inches deep and 3 inches wide to accommodate the roots and soil of the plant. Hold the pot upside down in one hand and tap it with the other hand until the root and soil slips out of the pot. Set the plant into the hole and fill in the hole with soil. Set the plant into the garden soil slightly deeper than it was in the pot.

Crop Families

The following vegetables are from the crop list and are grouped according to crop families using the most common vegetable in the group to represent the group.

CABBAGE FAMILY

Cabbage
Broccoli
Cauliflower
Collard
Kale
Brussels sprout

ONION FAMILY

Onion
Leek
Scallion
Chive

CARROT FAMILY

Carrot
Parsnip
Parsley
Celery

SQUASH FAMILY

Squash
Cucumber
Summer Squash

RADISH FAMILY

Radish
Daikon
Turnip
Rutabaga

MUSTARD FAMILY
Mustard
Brocolli rabe
Napa
Bok Choy
Augula
Mizuna

PEA/BEAN FAMILY

Pea
Stringbean

LETTUCE FAMILY

Lettuce
Burdock
Dandelion

MISCELANEOUS FAMILY

Sweet corn
Shiso
Shungiku

7.
Watering, Weeding and Mulching

Water is one of the essential foods of vegetables and all plants. The average quantity of water for garden vegetables is about one inch per week. Natural rainfall is the traditional way in which vegetable gardens receive water. Often natural rainfall will be sufficient for growing most vegetables in most parts of the world. Natural rainfall is the primary source of water. Secondary sources are:

1. Rain catch and tanks
2. Well
3. River or canal
4. Lake and pond
5. Spring

Rain catch and tanks is simply buckets, barrels, or tanks that hold rainwater as it flows off the roof of buildings. Place the tanks, barrels or buckets as close to the garden as possible or uphill from the garden so that the water can be transferred downhill naturally through a hose or pipe to the garden.

Many homes in the country have wells. This water is usually pulled up by an electric water pump, and can be extended to the garden by a hose. Gardeners may need to be careful not to use too much water for irrigation or the well may run low, making water for the home insufficient.

River water is also good for home gardens if it is not extremely contaminated. Water may be drawn from a river by buckets or by natural flow from a pipe placed upstream or by a pump.

Uncontaminated lake and pond water is also good for home gardens. It can be drawn by buckets or pumps to the garden.

A natural spring can also supply supplementary water to a vegetable garden. Spring water can be led to the garden by a pipe or a ditch and held in tanks or pools.

After a source of water is located and water is taken to a place near or in the garden, a method of applying the water is needed. Here are several methods:

1. Hand watering by watering can
2. By garden hose and/or sprinkler
3. By drip irrigation

Hand watering by watering can is the most simple and economical, yet is also the slowest and hardest. It may not be practical for very large gardens. With this method, the water is drawn from tanks, barrels, buckets, or hose, the source of which was a rain catch, a well, a river, canal, lake pond or spring. Pour the water through a kitchen type strainer to filter out small particles that may clog the small holes on the head of the watering can. The head of the watering can is called a "rose." Sprinkle water onto the vegetable plants, newly planted seeds, or transplants. The most important things to water are new transplants, newly planted seeds, and young sprouts. Large mature vegetables will survive better than small plants in times of scarce water due to their large root systems that draw water from deep in the soil. However, large mature plants will also benefit from extra water.

Apply water until the soil is well moistened. In times of hot, dry weather, watering is best in the evening because the water will soak into the soil overnight rather than evaporate as it will during the hot, sunny part of the day. Watering may not be necessary if the weather is cool, damp and rain is imminent.

Another way to water is by a hose, hand held or by mechanical lawn sprinkler.

Drip irrigation systems deliver water to the garden through a hose with many tiny holes. The water drips or seeps out at a slow and steady rate for many hours. These systems use a small volume of water and yet still supply a sufficient volume to the plants.

The source of water for drip irrigation can be from a tank or barrel at a higher elevation or from a hose pressurized from an electric pump. The systems work very well and are very useful in hot dry climates where water is scarce. They are, however, much more expensive than a common water can. They can be purchased from most farm and garden stores and mail order companies. (reference Chapter 13)

Mulch

In most of the wild and natural areas, such as forests and prairies, the soil is covered by a thick layer of dead plant material which has fallen from the living plants, such as tree leaves, grass, and weeds. This thick layer of dead plant material covers and protects the soil from drying out, washing or blowing away, and deep freezing. As it decomposes it enriches the soil. It also provides homes for many beneficial animals and insects. A thick mulch will inhibit new types of vegetation from growing under the original native plants. For example, the thick mulch of pine needles which accumulate under pine trees will inhibit foreign plants from growing close to pine trees.

In the vegetable garden it is beneficial to try to copy this natural phenomenon. Mulch in the garden will conserve moisture, therefore reducing the need to give supplemental water. It will conserve the soil by preventing washing away by rain and blowing away by wind. Mulch will inhibit weed growth and therefore reduce weeding. Mulch will improve the soil both by conserving it and by supplementing it with new fertility as it decomposes. One more benefit of mulch is that is provides food and protection for earthworms, toads, frogs, and beneficial insects.

Common materials used for mulch are grass, leaves, straw, sawdust, seaweed and grain hulls. Grass is one of the best mulches because it is frequently available and easy to use. Grass can be from freshly mowed grass clippings or old dry grass clippings of tall more mature grass. Grass which has mature seeds in it, such as hay, may contain many seeds which can readily sprout and become a big weed problem. This type of grass should be avoided.

Tree leaves are good for mulch. However, they may dry out and blow away. Leaves may be lightly covered with soil to prevent them from blowing away. Take this soil from the bed before mulching it with leaves.

Straw is the stalks of grain after the seed has been removed. It looks similar to hay, yet clean straw does not contain grass and weed seeds. Straw can be purchased from farms and farm stores.

Sawdust can be used for mulch. It is commonly available, inexpensive, clean and easy to work with. Old sawdust is better than fresh sawdust because it has lost its sap and has softened some, which makes it decompose more quickly and more compatible to the vegetables.

Seaweed such as kelp can be gathered from the beaches and used as mulch. The seaweed should be washed with water to remove excess salt which may harm young plants. Large quantities may be spread out on a road or lawn before a rainstorm to be washed off naturally.

Grain hulls are available in many parts of the world. Grain hulls make good mulch, although they blow away and attract many birds which may or may not be beneficial.

There are many other types of materials suitable for mulch, usually nearby the gardening area. Almost any stable organic material that is uniform and without weed seeds can be used for mulch, including compost and manure.

The basic methods for using mulch is to apply a thin cover over newly planted seeds, about 1/4 inch to 1/2 inch. A mulch over 1/2 inch-thick will inhibit the vegetable seeds from emerging. Apply the mulch evenly over the whole bed from edge to edge, and avoid making thick areas and bare areas. Water can be applied right over the mulch.

For newly transplanted vegetables, a thick mulch of about 2" can be applied around and in-between each plant. Water can be applied to the base of each plant on top of the mulch.

A thick mulch can be applied as a winter cover in areas with cold winters. Mulches may need to be removed prior to planting seeds in the spring. However, transplants can be put into the garden bed through the mulch by only moving the mulch at the place where the roots go into the soil. After vegetables are harvested and before new compost and seeds are applied, the old mulch may be removed and composted, or mixed into the soil by single digging. (Chapter 8)

Weeding

Originally there was no difference between vegetables and weeds. The origin of vegetables was from weeds. A plant which grows in the garden which is other than a vegetable may be called a weed.

Many weeds are edible, very few are poisonous, yet most are just unpalatable. Weeds can easily overcome new vegetable plants when the vegetables are young. Weeding is most important in the first four to six weeks after planting or transplanting.

There are several methods of weeding. The most efficient method is to walk down the path along side the bed and pull out the weeds by hand, or with the aid of a small trowel. Place the weeds in a five- gallon work bucket. When pulling it is beneficial to remove all the roots and shake off the soil. When the bucket becomes full or heavy it can be dumped into the compost. Weeds make very good compost because they contain leaf, stalk, roots, and soil. Double dug beds make weeding very easy, and the whole garden area can be reached due to the 4-foot-wide beds and system of pathways.

Another method of weeding is used when there are many small weed sprouts growing in-between the rows of vegetables. With a sharp and light-weight hoe, the weed sprouts are cut or chopped into the soil. The weed sprouts will then dry out and can be left right in the soil. This method works best when the weed sprouts are young and tender and still have shallow roots.

Strong perennial weeds must be removed with all their roots. One of the most difficult weeds is a perennial grass with roots that look like spaghetti. It is called by several names, one of which is quack grass.

Annual weeds which can produce hundreds of seeds per year should be pulled and composted before the seed matures.

The two most useful tools for weeding are a trowel and hoe. A special variety of weeding trowel is a "hori-hori" and a special sharp and light-weight hoe is a "collinear hoe". Both are available through mail order companies in the reference section.

8.
Harvesting

Harvesting vegetables is the most rewarding part of gardening. Harvest them at their peak ripeness. The more yang a vegetable is the longer its harvest period is and the more yin a vegetable is the shorter its harvest period is. For example, carrots are a more yang type vegetable. They can remain in the ground for several weeks after reaching a mature size. If winter comes they can remain in the soil for months, until spring. However, cucumbers, which are more yin, will remain in good eating condition for only a few days on the vine after which they expand, become yellow and watery. Unlike grain, bean and seeds that are harvested when the plant is "dead" and the seeds full and mature, vegetable "bodies" soft fruits and roots are eaten before they mature and bear seeds.

Tools needed for harvesting are: a heavy sharp knife, a trowel, pruning shears, and a box, bucket, or basket to hold the vegetables. Sometimes a fork or spade is helpful when harvesting root vegetables. Pre-washing the vegetables outside will help keep soil out of the kitchen.

Yin and Yang Guide to Vegetables

	YIN	YANG
Origin	Tropical	Temperate
Soil	Soft and wet	Firm and dry
Growing direction	Horizontally underground	Vertically downward
Growing speed	Faster	Slower
Size	Larger, expanded	Smaller, contracted
Height	Taller	Shorter
Texture	Softer	Harder
Color	Purple-blue-green-	-yellow-brown-orange-red
Chemical compound	More Potassium Less Sodium	Less Potassium More Sodium
Cooking time	Faster	Slower
Days to maturity	Faster	Slower
Height of growing crown	Higher	Lower
Number of crowns	Many	Few or one
Length of Fruits	Longer	Short or round
Resistance to freezing	No resistance to freezing temperatures	Resists freezing temperatures

Many vegetables can be harvested and eaten when young, if thinning is required or weather conditions necessitate an early harvest. The only vegetable which should not be harvested early is winter squash because it will not be sweet. It is, however, edible.

Some vegetables may produce buds and flowers prematurely or when left unharvested, these buds are edible and very delicious. Some common examples are Napa, daikon, bok choy, and mustard. These buds can be broken off, then the plant will produce more buds —similar to broccoli.

Many vegetables can be harvested in part or in whole. If harvested in part, the vegetable will continue to grow. The obvious examples are peas, string beans, summer squash, and cucumber. But lettuce, mustard, broccoli, broccoli mustard and bok choy can also be harvested in part, a little at a time, which will allow the plant to remain healthy and regrow.

The tops of many root vegetables are edible such as carrot, turnip, and radish. The exceptions are burdock, parsnip, and rutabaga. Replanting vegetables every 3 weeks will ensure a continuous harvest.

Surplus vegetables may be pickled, dried, and sometimes frozen or given to friends and family.

9.
Gardening Process Through the Season

Upon completion of double digging, the garden work becomes much easier. This is the process or sequence of gardening through the seasons:

1. Double dig (Chapter 3)
2. Plant (Chapter 6)
3. Water (Chapter 7)
4. Mulch (Chapter 7)
5. Weed (Chapter 7)
6. Harvest (Chapter 8)

Then:

First Option
1. Clean the bed
2. Add compost
3. Mix in compost

Second Option
1. Add compost
2. Single dig (or double dig)

Then:

Replant vegetables (spring and summer)
or plant cover crop (autumn)
or mulch heavily (winter)

First Option

This is the most common method used in small gardens to continue growing vegetables when the season is long enough to mature another crop. After the first crop has matured and been harvested, strip that bed, or a portion of that bed, clean of all plant materials such as weeds, mulch, and vegetable waste. This material is called "field trash" in farming terminology.

Then take the field trash to the composting area where it will begin decomposing. Apply mature compost of a fine grade or texture to the soil of the garden bed at the rate of 2 inches to 4 inches. Two inches is suitable for soils which are of good quality and 4 inches for soils which are still poor or weak in fertility. Mix this compost into the soil by any of the following three methods:

1. "Spading"—Using a shovel, dig into the soil and compost, lift the material out and turn it over, dumping the compost into the hole first with the soil on top. Repeat this digging and dumping motion about every foot.

This method is called spading although a shovel is used instead of a spade. Some compost may remain on top of the soil and the bed may have a rough, uneven surface. Use a steel rake to level the surface of the bed the same as is done in the last step of double digging.

2. "Forking"—Insert a spading fork, such as the one used in double digging, into the soil and compost, then lift and turn the soil/compost over. Repeat this inserting and turning about every foot in the same general pattern as the spading. Then rake the bed smooth.

3. "Cultivating"—Using a cultivator or a hoe, strike or chop the soil/compost about every foot in the same general pattern as spading and forking. Then rake the bed smooth.

The soil and compost conditions determine the method as well as the gardeners' preference of tools. The goal of spading, forking and cultivating is to mix compost into the soil to make fertile soil with a clean smooth surface suitable for planting.

Second Option

This method is used when the garden is very large, which makes hauling all the "field trash" to the compost area difficult. Single digging is similar to double digging, but is easier and faster. Two people can prepare and single dig a 25-foot bed in 1 hour. Single digging step by step:

1. Cover the whole bed with 3 to 4 inches of compost.
2. Remove the field trash and compost from the first trench, place this in buckets. It will fit into about three 5-gallon buckets.
3. Remove about 6 inches of topsoil from the first trench, and put it into a wheelbarrow. If there is a large volume of field trash and compost, remove more than 6 inches of top soil to make a deeper trench. The line between the bed and the path should be made straight and distinct with a shovel.
4. Pull or scrape the field trash and compost from the second trench into the bottom of the first trench.
5. With a shovel, put about 6 inches of topsoil from the second trench on top of the field trash and compost in the first trench. Cover all the field trash completely and distribute the soil evenly on the first trench.
6. With a shovel, pull or scrape the field trash and compost from the third trench into the second trench, then cover the field trash with about 6 inches of topsoil from the third trench. This is the process that was done to the first trench.
7. Continue in this way to the last trench, then add the field trash and compost from the buckets into the trench and cover it with the topsoil from the wheelbarrow.
8. With a steel rake, rake the bed smooth. All field trash should be buried and the bed and pathways surrounding the bed should be straight and distinct.

Rather than single digging a bed may be double dug by cultivating the field trash and compost into the subsoil.

Again, merely cultivate and add compost to the subsoil.

Upon completion of cleaning the bed and mixing in compost (first option) or single digging in the field trash and compost (second option), the gardener may replant vegetables by direct planting seeds or transplanting small plants, if there is enough growing season left to mature a crop. Vegetables may be replanted during the spring and summer in most places.

If the season is too short to mature another crop of vegetables, such as in autumn, a cover crop may be planted. Cover crops are crops which are planted for the purpose of helping the soil rather than for harvest and consumption. Cover crops protect the soil from erosion and drying out, control weeds by covering the soil, and add fertility when they are dug into the soil.

Here is a list of common cover crops and planting times:

• buckwheat - summer
• millet - summer
• clover - late summer or spring
• oats - late summer or spring
• rye - autumn
• mustard - spring

Cover crop seeds are broadcast lightly over the smoothly finished bed, about 1 seed per 2 inches, and lightly raked into the soil, a light mulch of grass is sometimes helpful to help the cover crop get started yet it is not always necessary. Rye is the most hardy cover crop for late plantings in the north. The cover crop may remain in the garden until the bed is to be used for planting vegetables the next spring, at that time it must be single dug or double dug into the soil to allow the vegetables to be planted.

If the season is too short or cold to plant vegetables or a cover crop then a heavy mulch of seedless grass or leaves is very helpful in protecting the soil during winter until planting time in spring. To keep leaves from blowing away sprinkle soil on top of them. The heavy mulch may be completely removed in spring to plant seeds, or single dug into the soil, or transplant young plants through the mulch. The old mulch makes a good addition to the compost pile.

There are methods of extending the growing season both in spring and in autumn. In some climates, vegetables will grow all year naturally and in other areas vegetables will grow all year with some kind of protection.

A large volume of good quality vegetables may be grown without these seemingly artificial aids, yet more can be grown with them. They are not essential, only helpful.

Single Digging Diagram

Side View

Remove	step #4	Compost	and field trash (step#1)	
Remove topsoil (step #3)	step #5			
step #4 subsoil				

1. Row covers are a lightweight material which float above the vegetables. They allow sun and rain to enter and raise the temperature a few degrees. They also exclude insects. This added protection and warmth helps seeds to germinate and grow quickly in early spring and can keep the autumn frost off beans, cucumbers and other frost tender crops, thereby extending their harvest another two to three weeks. Another type of row cover is a heavier type which is supported on hoops. It creates more heat than the floating type. These are offered through most garden seed catalogs. (see reference)

2. A cold frame is a structure with a glass or clear plastic cover which allows sunlight to enter and warm the plants and soil inside of the structure. Cold frames face south to receive maximum sunlight. The angle of the cover should be about 45 degrees. A cold frame may be made simply from a window and boards, or purchased from a garden or farm store, or a mail order company.

3. Hot frames are cold frames with an additional source of heat inside the frame. The traditional source of heat for hot frames was a deep pile of fresh horse manure, which during decomposing, gave off heat. A modern source of heat is electricity, something similar to an electric blanket. These electric heating pads are also available through garden and farm stores and mail order companies.

Cold frames and hot frames are not essential to home gardening. Many good crops can be grown without them, although they will help produce vegetables earlier and later in a cold climate.

4. Greenhouses, both attached to a house and separate, offer the gardener more options to grow vegetables. Flats can be started in them and vegetables can be grown entirely in them from early spring to late autumn in cold climates and year round in places with moderate winters with only the sun to heat.

Inexpensive plastic and wood greenhouse kits in various sizes and shapes from large to small are available. Greenhouses can also be used for drying vegetables after harvest, such as onions and squash, and drying other food products such as cut dried daikon (Chapter 12) and for drying vegetable seeds. (Chapter 11)

Of all the season extending methods and structures, an inexpensive greenhouse is the most useful and efficient for a wide variety of uses. These are available through mail order companies. (Ref. Chapter 14)

10.
Summary of Factors That Create Good Crops

There are seven factors that, if managed well, will create good crops and a large volume of delicious food. These factors are:

1. Sun
2. Soil
3. Water
4. Timing and method of planting
5. Type and variety of crop (seed)
6. Weed control
7. Animal, insect and disease control

Planning a garden in an area that receives ample sunlight is very important. (Chapter 2)

Double digging method can change even the most poor hard soil into rich fertile soil. (Chapter 5)

Water is essential for all plants and animals. The correct quantity will produce healthy vegetables. (Chapter 6)

These three factors are primary. Without them, vegetables will not grow well. Areas with good soil and sun but no water become deserts. Areas with plenty of water and sun and no soil are ponds, rivers or oceans, and areas with plenty of water and good soil yet very little sun are the polar regions. Although plants do grow under these difficult conditions, they are not normally used for food crops.

Timing and method of planting is very important. (Chapter 6) For example, if all other factors are good for crop growth and squash is planted late, perhaps in July, then the squash will not mature because the growing season is too short. Method of planting refers to depth, spacing, thinning, transplanting, and mulch. (Chapters 6 and 7) The size of a seed determines the depth of planting. In general, plant large seeds more deeply and small seeds more shallowly. The size of the mature plant determines the final spacing. The larger the mature plant, the greater the final spacing is. Thinning is used when seeds are planted close together. Some of the small plants are removed to allow the remaining plants to grow large. This method insures that the whole garden space will be filled with plants regardless of how good or poor germination is. For example:

Vegetable Thinning

1. Carrot seed planted 1 per inch

2. Young carrots, roots, and leaf are touching
remove every other carrot

3. Large mature carrots at 1-2" spacing

These remaining carrots can grow to full mature size without any further thinning. The small carrots thinned out can be eaten. Thinning is used frequently with directly planted seeds, usually root crops, and in flats planting when two seeds are planted per pot. It is important to thin when the plants leaves begin to touch each other. If the thinning is delayed too long, all the plants will become thin, pale and weak from lack of direct sunlight.

Some crops, such as broccoli, may be either direct planted or transplanted. The method a gardener chooses may determine the success of the crop. The transplant method, in general, is more successful than direct planting for upward growing vegetables, because the primary factors of sun, soil and water can be managed carefully in the flats where as they can not always be managed as well in the open garden.

The type and variety of crop chosen can determine a successful harvest or failure, even if all other factors are well managed. For example, if tropical melons and artichokes are planted in the far north, it is probable that the crops will not mature. More suitable crops would be cucumbers and cabbage.

Within a single type of crop there are many varieties; the gardener should select the variety which best fits the environment and his personal taste. For example, sweet corn has many varieties. There are varieties which mature in 70 days and varieties which mature in 110 days. Gardeners in the south with a long season can grow a 110- day sweet corn, yet that variety may not be successful in the north with a 90-day frost free summer. The calendar and planting chart will help to determine which crops will be successful. (Chapter 6)

Weed control is an important factor in creating a bountiful harvest of vegetables. (Chapter 7) Some of the weeds can be eaten in small quantities. Some of the more common are lambs quarters, dandelion, wild amaranth, plantain and chick weed. Weeds and other wild plants should be properly identified before eating.

Wild and domestic animals enjoy eating vegetable gardens. Animals which eat vegetables are moles, rabbits, chickens, woodchucks, raccoons, deer and birds. Animals such as dogs and cats may also disturb the garden.

The most effective way to prevent animals from eating

the entire garden is to build a fence around it. (Chapter 2) Determine which animals are present then consult the local farm, garden or hardware store for suitable fencing. One type of fence will usually keep several types of animals out. Fences are not very expensive and can look attractive if properly made. Regardless of what type of fence or other protection is used, it is common and natural to lose some crops to animals.

Insect control begins with creating and maintaining good soil, sunlight, and correct water levels. When these three primary factors are managed well, vegetables will be in optimum health and insect damage will be minimal. It is natural to lose about 10 percent of the total crop to insects because the plant and animal kingdom are inseparable.

Immature compost, fresh manure, and vegetable waste left in the garden may encourage insect problems. Single digging will bury these materials, clean up the garden and reduce insect problems.

Some insects thrive during hot, dry conditions (yang environment). Apply cold water to vegetables to reduce these insects. Some insects thrive in cold wet conditions. (yin environment) To correct this insect problem, remove mulch, thin the plants and apply wood ash to the soil (make the environment more yang).

Another method of insect control is to hand-pick the insects off the vegetables and remove them to another place. This only works for large, slow moving insects. There are some natural insecticides available from garden stores and seed companies. These insecticides are usually derived from plants and are safe to use on vegetables. These are used as a last resort.

Beneficial insects such as ladybugs are now sold by garden and seed companies. Ladybugs eat many insects which eat vegetables. Birds which eat insects can be attracted to the home garden by setting up bird houses and drinking water. Bats also eat insects and can be encouraged to live near the garden by building bat houses. Crop rotation can also reduce insect damage. Crop rotation means changing the location of crops each year so that the same crop family does not occupy the same place two years in a row. A simple example is:

Crop Rotation Chart

4 beds	Carrot Family	Onion Family	1st year
	Cabbage Family	Squash Family	
	Cabbage Family	Carrot Family	2nd year
	Squash Family	Onion Family	
	Squash Family	Cabbage Family	3 year
	Onion Family	Carrot Family	
	Onion Family	Squash Family	4th year
	Carrot Family	Cabbage Family	

Crop rotation will reduce insect damage, disease problems and depletion of nutrients in soil. Yet, crop rotation need not be followed absolutely because there may be times when two different crop families may grow in the same soil in one year, or new crops may be introduced or various other factors may alter the crop rotation plan. Crop rotation is a general guideline.

Disease control is managed similarly to insect control by creating good sun, soil and water conditions, crop rotation, and by avoiding immature compost and fresh manures near planting time.

Each year in the garden there will be successful harvest and "crop failures." The "crop failures" are not entirely failures. From these experiences the gardener can learn which factor or combination of factors were unbalanced. Crop failures can be pulled out, composted, and the garden space can be refertilized and replanted to a different crop, thereby turning failure into a bountiful harvest.

11.
Forestry for the Home Garden

Trees are very important to human, plant, and animal life. Forestry is the art of managing trees to create the maximum health of trees, thereby also benefiting other plants, animals and humans.

Frequently, trees which grow around roads, buildings, fields, walls and rivers are neglected. Neglected trees begin to grow too close to each other causing unnatural shapes and eventually disease or decline in health. Trees are created by more yin force from earth so they naturally expand upwards and outwards. When trees grow too close together, they obstruct each other as they expand, just like vegetables if planted too close together.

The first part of forestry for the home garden is selective thinning. Selective thinning involves cutting the inferior trees around the periphery of the garden, in favor of the strong healthy trees. Lower branches which interfere with the garden are also cut. This cutting opens the garden area making it larger and brighter and at the same time improves the remaining trees.

Selective thinning greatly enlarges and improves the garden and should be done as a first step in preparing a garden.

As a general guideline, the larger the tree the greater the distance should be in between. When the branches of two trees begin to touch and overlap, one tree can be cut. Small trees, up to 4" diameter, can be cut with a hand saw. Trees larger than that are more easily cut with a chain saw. If the home gardener does not own or wish to operate a chain saw, a local tree company can do the tree work.

The trees which are cut can be used for firewood. The branches may be stacked in an unused place or shredded by a tree company or cut into small pieces for firewood. The last choice for removing branches is to burn them, for this makes unnecessary air pollution and destroys organic material valuable to the soil.

Selective Thinning for Trees

Planting and Thinning Trees (Top View)

1. Young cedar trees are planted for a windbreak 5' apart

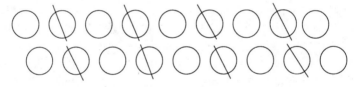

2. When the trees begin to touch, every other tree may be cut

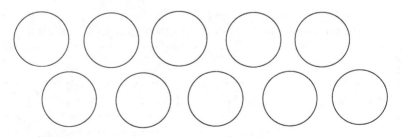

3. Large, full, mature cedar trees

4. Side view, remove every other tree to allow proper tree growth

The second part of forestry involves planting trees. Trees can be planted to block the cold winds, for food and for beauty. Trees should not be planted where they will block the sun to the garden, and trees should be at least 15 ft. from the garden because their roots will reach into the garden.

Selective thinning and tree planting is done every few years as trees grow and expand.

12.
Vegetable Storage

In the warmer areas of the South, vegetables can be grown all year. However, in the North ,vegetables were traditionally preserved and stored in three ways and, more recently, in two other ways. The three traditional methods were cold storage in a root cellar, drying and pickling. The more recent methods are canning and freezing.

Cold storage in a root cellar is a good method for storing many crops from the garden. The crops which store well are burdock, cabbage, carrot, daikon, parsnip, and rutabaga. These crops keep well in cool, moist, dark condition about 35-45° F., or 2° C. Squash and onions keep well in cool, dry, dark conditions about 45-50° F., or 8° C.

The root vegetables should not be washed before storage. The water may encourage mold and spoilage. Sort the vegetables and store only the best vegetables that do not have bruises or cuts. The less than perfect vegetables can be washed and cooked within a few weeks, before they spoil. The good root vegetables can be laid in boxes in between layers of clean, moist sand or sawdust.

Cabbage can be set side by side, not touching, on a shelf with their outer leaves still attached. Squash and onions can be stored together, squash side by side (not touching), and onions in boxes.

Vegetables in storage can spoil in two different ways. The first way is by overly yin conditions that cause rotting, mold and sprouting. The problem is usually too much moisture and dirty conditions in the storage room with a lack of ventilation. The other way is by overly yang conditions in the storage room; it may be too dry and bright. Under these conditions the vegetables dry out and shrivel up. Soaking root vegetables in water overnight will expand them, however, then they must be used in cooking.

Keep the root cellar clean and check all vegetables in storage weekly to quickly find any vegetable that has begun to spoil. Use these vegetables in that days' cooking. One vegetable left to spoil can spoil the whole box. Under proper storage conditions, vegetables can keep well until spring.

Drying vegetables is another traditional method of storage before modern canning, freezing and importation began. Most vegetables can be dried. Some are more delicious and practical to dry than others. Here are four examples of vegetables that are easy and practical to dry.

Daikon—"Kiri-boshi Daikon," shredded and dried daikon, is used frequently in macrobiotic cooking and is very delicious and beneficial to people's health. Select large, firm, and sweet daikon, wash and dry well, shred the daikon on a box grater on the side with the large holes. It will appear as short, white ribbons. Four or five medium-size roots of shredded daikon will fill a platter. Wood platters and bamboo mats are best. Plastic platters and metal platters are least desirable because they will alter the flavor of the daikon. Dry the shredded daikon in the sun. If the sun is strong, soon the top parts of the shredded daikon will become dry. Mix the moist and dry shreds together and then spread them out again. Take the daikon in at night or in rainy or damp weather. Continue to dry and mix until just before the daikon shreds become hard. Depending upon weather, this may take three days. The final drying can be done in an oven on very low heat, about 100 degrees F., or near a wood stove. the finished product can be stored in a paper bag. Properly prepared "Kire boshi Daikon" will keep well until the new crop of daikon grows in the next year.

Parsley, chives, and shiso are all prepared the same. Harvest and then lay in a single layer on wood platters, bamboo mats, screens, or plastic trays in a dry and well ventilated area away from direct sunlight. Strong direct sunlight will bleach the delicate leaves and alter the flavor. Drying time may take three to five days, then, if thoroughly dried, the leaves may be stored in jars and used all winter until the new crop grows in the spring. The dry leaves can be stored whole or crushed, the hard stems of parsley and shiso can be discarded.

The other traditional method of vegetable storage is pickling. Fermented food aids in digestion; about a teaspoon of pickle per meal is sufficient. Nearly all vegetables can be pickled, some are more delicious and practical than others. Salt is the material which preserves the vegetable. The salt enters the vegetable through time and pressure. The salt replaces some of the water in the vegetable. The most common vegetables to pickle are Daikon radish, Napa cabbage, green cabbage and cucumber. Pickle recipes are in the food processing book. (reference) The pickle crocks should be stored in a cool, dry and clean place and covered tightly with paper or cloth to keep out contamination.

The more modern methods of preservation like canning and freezing vegetables are less desirable than fresh, cold storage, drying and pickling, yet some home garden vegetables may be canned or frozen for occasional use through the winter months.

When each region's agriculture, food storage and food processing develop properly—with many farms and gardens—fresh, local, organic vegetables will become available all year round.

13.
Recipes

These are some simple and delicious ways of cooking fresh garden vegetables. The vegetables are from the crop list (Chapter 6). The recipes are simple and condensed. For complete macrobiotic cooking, see the recommended reading list at the end.

1. Broccoli—Quickly boil in water without salt; broth can be drunk like tea
2. Broccoli mustard—Quickly sauté in dark sesame oil with a dash of shoyu
3. Burdock and carrot kimpira—Cut equal volumes of burdock and carrot into shoestrings and sauté in dark sesame oil and sea salt for about 20 minutes
4. Cabbage-Cut one-half green cabbage into wedges and cook with one spoon of umeboshi paste in 1/2 inch of water, cook until core is soft
5. Carrot and parsnip nishime—Cut two carrots and two parsnips in large pieces, cook in 1 inch of water with a 2-inch strip of kombu, one shiitake and a few pinches of sea salt. Cook in a covered pot until soft or water evaporates, about 20 minutes
6. Cauliflower—Quickly boil in 1/2 inch of water without salt
7. Collards—Quickly boil in 1 inch of water without salt. The broth can be drunk like tea

8. Daikon—nishime-Cut one large daikon into large 1 inch slices, cook in 1 inch of water with a 2 inch piece of kombu for 15 minutes, add a dash of shoyu and cook 5 minutes more. This can also be cooked together with about 1/2 of the green leaves. Cut the leaves into 1 inch length pieces and add after the first 10 minutes of cooking the root.

9. Kale—Quickly boil in 1 inch of water without salt. The broth can be drunk like tea.

10. Leek—Cut into 2 inch length pieces and boil about 3-4 minutes in 1 inch of water, without salt. The broth can be drunk.

11. Napa—Cook the same as broccoli, collard, kale, and leeks

12. Onion— Sauté in corn or sesame oil until soft. Season with sea salt and serve as a condiment to rice or millet

13. Scallion—Cut small and served raw as a condiment to miso soup or noodles in broth

14. (1) Squash nishime—Cut one squash into large pieces, cook 25 minutes in 1 inch of water with a 2-inch piece of kombu and a pinch of salt, in a covered pot. Cook until squash is soft and water has evaporated.

(2). Baked squash—Take one small whole squash, wash skin, poke 3-4 holes into center of squash, rub outside with sesame oil and sea salt, bake in a ceramic pot with a cover at 200° F. for 1 hour or until soft. Turn squash occasionally. The squash can also be baked upon a wood stove in a ceramic pot, for 2 hours.

15. Sweet corn—Remove husk and boil in 1 inch of water for 6-8 minutes or until most of the water evaporates

16. Bok choy—Quickly boil in 1 inch of water without salt. Broth can be drunk as a tea

17. Brussels sprout nishime—Cut an X into the stem of the sprout to help it cook well inside. Cook sprouts in 1 inch of water with a piece of kombu for 20 minutes in a covered pot. Add miso at the end of cooking.

18. Celery condiment—Cut celery stalk and leaf into small pieces. Sauté in toasted sesame oil for about 10 minutes. Add shoyu after 5 minutes. Serve with rice and other grains.

19. Cucumber with wakame—Slice cucumbers. Soak wa-

kame in water 5-10 minutes then cut in small pieces. Mix with salt and let sit for 30 minutes to 1 hour. Mix wakame with cucumber, add shoyu and rice vinegar. Serve cool.

20. Lettuce—pressed salad-Wash, cut and mix lettuce with other fresh garden vegetables such as radish, cucumber, scallion, celery, chive, parsley, arugula or shiso. Mix in sea salt and place in a ceramic bowl with a pressing weight for about 1-2 hours. Wash off salt if the salt is excessive and serve.

21. Mizuna—This mustard like vegetable is very delicious when cut into 2-inch long pieces and sautéed in dark sesame oil and shoyu for about 5 minutes

22. Mustard—Red mustard can be prepared like mizuna. Sauté in dark sesame oil and shoyu for about 5 minutes. Green mustards are good lightly boiled like kale, collards, bok choy and other greens. The cooking broth may be too pungent to drink

23. Parsley—As a garnish to sweet soups and sweet dishes such as squash soup and parsnip nishime

24. Peas—Green peas in soft rice make delicious breakfast cereal. Using firm rice left over from dinner, add shelled green peas at the last 10 minutes of cooking of the soft rice.

Snow peas—Stir fry with onion and noodles. Sauté sliced onions in dark sesame oil until they are soft. Add snow peas and sauté 1-2 minutes.Add cooked udon, soba or whole wheat spaghetti. Add shoyu and stir fry 2-3 minutes. Serve hot with strips of nori and grated ginger.

Snap peas—Lightly boil with equal volumes of carrots in 1 inch of water and a pinch of sea salt until soft. This is especially good with new baby carrots cut to the same size as the snap peas.

25. Radish— Wash and lightly boil whole roots with tops attached in 1 inch of water for about 3-5 minutes with or without sea salt. The small thin tap root may be cut off and discarded before cooking if it is hard. Serve radishes whole as part of a light breakfast or lunch.

26. Rutabaga-nishime—Wash and cut roots into large pieces. Boil in 1 inch of water with kombu in a covered pot for about 20-30 minutes or until soft and water evaporates. Add

sea salt at the beginning of cooking or mix at the end of cooking.

27. Stringbean with almonds—Cut each stringbean into 2 or 3 pieces and sauté in sesame oil with sea salt for about 4-5 minutes. After cooking, mix with roasted and sliced almonds. The ratio may be about 60-70 percent stringbeans to 30-40 percent almonds.

28. Summer squash—Slice a small squash lengthwise and pan fry each side 2-3 minutes with 1/4 inch water or toasted sesame oil with a pinch of sea salt on each piece of squash

29. Arugula—This pungent Italian green is a relative of the mustard family and is delicious lightly boiled like the other greens

30. Chive—Use as a garnish for salty type soups like miso or noodle broth. Cut into small pieces and serve raw on top.

31. Dandelion—Wash the roots and greens of wild or domestic dandelion and cut both into small pieces. Sauté in sesame oil about 5 minutes, then add miso diluted in a little water and cook 10 minutes. Add roasted sesame seed and serve over rice or other cooked grains as a condiment.

32. Shiso—Red or green varieties are delicious in quick and lightly pickled recipes such as shiso and green cabbage or turnip and shiso pickles.

33. Shungiku—This Japanese edible Chrysanthemum has very delicious green leaves which can be lightly boiled like other greens.

Fresh garden vegetables properly cooked and eaten will make a person harmonious with their environment by naturally adjusting their body condition to the weather, soil, water, air, and sunlight around them.

Appendix

Standard Macrobiotic Dietary Guidelines*

Foods for Daily Consumption

• **Whole Cereal Grains:** The principal food of each meal is ideally whole cereal grain, comprising from 50 to 60 percent of the total volume. Whole grains include brown rice, whole wheat berries, barley, millet, and rye, as well as corn, buckwheat, and other botanically similar plants. From time to time, whole grain products, such as cracked wheat, rolled oats, noodles, pasta, bread, baked goods, and other unrefined flour products, may be served as part of this volume.

• **Soup:** One to two small bowls of soup, making up about 5 to 10 percent of daily food intake, are consumed each day. The soup broth is made frequently with miso or tamari soy sauce and also includes vegetable, bean, and grain soups.

• **Vegetables:** About 25 to 30 percent of daily food includes fresh vegetables prepared in a variety of ways, including steaming, boiling, baking, sautéing, salads, and marinades. The vegetables include a variety of root vegetables (such as turnip, carrots, and daikon radish), ground vegetables (such as onions and fall- and winter-season squashes), and leafy green vegetables (such as kale, collard greens, broccoli, turnip greens, mustard greens, and watercress).

• **Beans and Sea Vegetables:** A small portion, about 10 percent by volume, of daily food intake includes cooked beans such as adzukis, lentils, and chickpeas or bean products such as tofu, tempeh, and natto and sea vegetables, including kombu, wakame, nori, dulse, hijiki, and arame.

• **Seasoning and Oil:** Naturally processed sea salt is used in seasoning, along with miso, tamari soy sauce, umeboshi, brown rice vinegar, fresh grated ginger and other traditional items. Naturally processed, unrefined vegetable oil is recommended for daily cooking such as dark sesame seed oil. Kuzu is commonly used for gravies and sauces.

• **Condiments:** Condiments include gomashio (roasted sesame salt), roasted seaweed powders, umeboshi plums, tekka root vegetable, and many others.

• **Pickles:** A small volume of home-made pickles is eaten each day to aid in digestion of grains and vegetables.

• **Beverages:** Spring or well water is used for drinking, preparing tea, and for general cooking. Bancha twig tea (also known as kukicha) is the most commonly served beverage, though roasted barley tea, and other grain-based teas or traditional, nonstimulant herbal teas are also used frequently.

Occasional Foods for Those in Usual Good Health

• **Animal Food:** A small volume of white-meat fish or seafood may be eaten a few times per week.

• **Seeds and Nuts:** Seeds and nuts, lightly roasted and salted with sea salt or seasoned with tamari soy sauce, may be enjoyed as occasional snacks.

• **Fruit:** Fruit may be taken a few times a week, preferably cooked or naturally dried, as a snack or dessert, provided the fruit grows in the local or similar climate zone.

• **Dessert:** Occasional desserts may consist of cookies, pudding, cake, pie, and other dishes made with naturally sweet foods such as apples, fall and winter squashes, azuki beans, or dried fruit or may be sweetened with a natural grain-based sweetener such as rice syrup, barley malt, or amasake.

* These guidelines are for four-season temperate climates of the world including most of the United States, Europe, the U.S.S.R., and China. Recommendations will vary for colder, polar or semi-polar regions and for warmer, tropical or subtropical climates and environments. Way of eating suggestions also include preparing food in an attractive manner, eating with a calm, peaceful mind, and thorough chewing.

Resources

Seeds

Best sources for northern gardeners

Johnny's—full line of macrobiotic vegetable seeds, also tools, supplies, and books. Johnny's, Foss Hill Rd., Albion, ME 04910-9731. 207-437-4301.

Abundant Life—organic seeds all non hybrid, best seeds for northwest and west coast, also books. Abundant Life, P. O. Box 772, 1022 Lawrence St., Port Townsend, WA 98368.

Burpee's—many good varieties of seeds, good for north and south areas, supplies also. Burpee's, W. Atlee Burpeee and Co., Warminster, PA 18974. 800-888-1447.

Tools

Smith and Hawken—English spading forks, spades and supplies, many top quality tools. Smith and Hawken, 2 Arbor Lane, Box 6900, Florence, KY 41022-6900. 800-776-3336.

A.M. Leonard—full line of tools and supplies for gardening, forestry and yard. A. M. Leonarrd, 241 Fox Drive, P.O. Box 816, Piqua, OH 45356. 800-433-0633.

Peaceful Valley Farm Supply—good tools and supplies especially for the west coast. P.V.F.S., P.O. Box 2209, Grass

Valley, CA 95945. 916-272-4769.

Mellinger—supplies, tools and seeds for the Midwest. Mellinger, 2310 W. South Range Rd., North Lima, OH 44452-9731. 216-549-9861.

Books

1. *How to Grow More Vegetables* by John Jeavons, Ten Speed Press, 1991.
2. *Four Season Harvest* by Elliot Coleman,Chelsea Green, 1992.
3. *Organic Gardening* by Robert Rodale, Rodale Press, 1971.
4. *Seed Starters Handbook* by Nancy Babul, Rodale Press, 1988.
5. *The Book of Macrobiotics* by Michio Kushi with Alex Jack, Japan Publications, revised edition, 1986.
6. *The Macrobiotic Way* by Michio Kushi, Avery Publishishing Group, 1986.
7. *Macrobiotic Diet* by Michio and Aveline Kushi, Japan Publications, 1985.
8. *Macrobiotic Home Food Processing* by Guy Lalumiere, One Peaceful World Press, 1993.
9. *Standard Macrobiotic Diet* by Michio Kushi, One Peaceful World Press, 1992.

For further information on books and publications, contact One Peaceful World Press, P.O. Box 10, Becket, MA USA 01223, (413) 623-2322.

For further study of macrobiotic cooking, philosophy, shiatsu, gardening, exercise and food processing, contact the Kushi Institute, P.O. Box 7, Becket, MA USA 01223, (413) 623-5741.

Glossary

Agriculture—The art and method of cultivating the earth to produce food, fiber, fuel, lumber and other useful materials

Bed—A raised section of garden or field soil where the crop is planted, usually 2-4 feet wide and any length over 3 feet

Burdock—A root vegetable that grows 2-3 feet long with large broad green leaves. A member of the composit family

Compost—A mixture of organic matter and minerals fermented and condensed which is used to improve soil and fertilize plants

Cover Crop—Plants which are grown and not harvested but rather plowed into the soil for the purpose of building soil fertility, controlling weeds, disease, insects and soil erosion

Crop—Plants intentionally grown and harvested for use as food, fiber, fuel, lumber and other uses beneficial to humans, animals or soil

Cultivation—1. A light and shallow mixing of garden or field soil for the purpose of controlling weeds, mixing compost or fertilizer into the soil or to cover seeds with soil 2. Agriculture, i.e., the art and method of growing crops

Direct Planting—A method of planting by which seeds are placed directly into the garden soil

Double Digging—A method of cultivating garden soil in which both the subsoil and topsoil are loosened and fertilized

Fertilizer—A material added to the soil which increases the nutrition as a benefit to plants

Field Trash—Any organic material left on a garden bed after harvest, i.e., weeds, mulch, vegetable waste

Flat—Trays of potted plants for transplanting

Forking—A method of cultivating garden soil with a spading fork to loosen soil, remove stones or mix compost into the soil

Furrow—A straight narrow and usually shallow line or trench made in a garden or field for the purpose of planting seeds

Kombu—A sea vegetable similar to kelp

Leaching—The washing away of nutrients, especially nitrogen, from the soil by water

Limestone—A natural, white, sandy-like material made from crushed white stone high in calcium and magnesium

Miso—A salty paste made from fermented soybean, grain and salt

Mulch—Any organic material placed on top of the garden soil which protects the soil from drying and erosion, and prevents weed growth

Nitrogen—(N) A primary soil element essential to plant growth, which creates large, green leaves

Phosphorus—(P) A primary soil element essential to plant growth which creates strong stems and fruits

Plowing—A method of cultivating soil, usually by a mold board plow

Potassium—(K) A primary soil element essential for plant growth which creates strong roots

Shiso—A leafy vegetable red or green in color and member of the mint family

Shungiku—A leafy vegetable and member of the Chrysanthemum family

Single digging—A method of cultivating garden soil in which field trash is buried into the top soil thereby enrichening it and cleaning the surface of the soil

Spading—A method of cultivating garden soil with a shovel to loosen or mix in compost

Standard macrobiotic diet—A traditional way of eating based upon whole grains, bean and vegetables

Thinning—The process of removing excess plants or trees to allow more space for the remaining plants to grow

Tillage—The cultivation of soil, i.e., double digging, single digging, forking, plowing, etc.

Transplanting—A method of planting by which seeds are planted in pots for flats and later moved to the garden soil

Wakame—A sea vegetable which is dark green and leaf-like

Weeds—A plant which is naturally occurring in a garden or field which may diminish the yield of an intentionally planted crop

Yang—The energy tendency that is contracting inward and downward

Yin—The energy tendency that is expanding upward and outward

About the Author

Masato Mimura (Chris Fry) was born and raised in Rhode Island. He has developed agriculture at the Kushi Institute since 1986, primarily growing organic vegetables. He lives with his wife, Mariko, in Becket, Massachusetts.